19.95

RISE OF THE GIG LEADERS

WHY INTERIM LEADERS
ARE VITAL IN TODAY'S ORGANIZATIONS

NEIL GRANT

outskirts
press

Table of Contents

Foreword i

Introduction v

About the Author xiii

PART I: Today's Interim Leaders

Chapter 1: Why Interim Leaders? 3

   Changing Organizational Models 4

   Leadership Options and the Interim Advantage 7

   Interim Strengths and Misperceptions 10

   Interim v. Consultant 12

   Geographic Perspective on Markets 14

Chapter 2: What Clients Say 18

Chapter 3: What Interims Say 29

   Shifting Mindsets 30

   Interim Testimonials 32

PART II: The DNA of Interim Leaders

Chapter 4: The SCILL Model© 41

   Case Study: Create Brand Strategy 44

Chapter 5: Savvy 47

    Organizational Savvy 48

    Relational Savvy 52

    Cultural Savvy 58

    Case Study: Restructure Business and
    Build for Future Growth 62

Chapter 6: Critical 65

    Crisis or Turnaround Management....................70

    Organizational Growth 73

    Integration Following a Merger or Acquisition 75

    Reducing Cost and Increasing Value....................77

    Raising the Bar on Performance and Expectations 79

    Case Study: Roll-out of CRM (Customer Relationship
    Management) System 81

Chapter 7: Impact...84

    Dynamic Impact 88

    Insightful Impact 90

    Results-focused Impact....................................93

    Courageous Impact 95

    Case Study: Business Turnaround 97

Chapter 8: Leadership..101

    Personal Leadership 103

    Situational Leadership....................................106

    Transformational Leadership 109

    Inspirational Leadership 112

Reputational Leadership..116

Case Study: Systems Upgrade...................................117

Chapter 9: Legacy..120

Organizations 122

Projects..125

People..127

Case Study: Revitalize Integrated Business &
HR Strategy & Culture Change Program 130

Part III:The Value of Interim Leaders

Chapter 10: Interims and Change 135

Scope of Change...137

Politics of Change 141

Speed of Change...142

Communication of Change 145

Embedding Change...147

Chapter 11: The Interim as Coach and Mentor..............150

The Interim as Coach 153

The Interim as Mentor 156

Chapter 12: GREAT Interim Competencies 160

Gravitas 162

Resilience 164

Engagement 165

Attitude (to excel)..168

Transformational 169

Part IV: Engaging Interim Leaders

Chapter 13: Hiring Interims 173

Timeframe..174

Finding Interims 176

Multiple Clients...178

Relationships..179

Chapter 14: The Contract...184

Psychological...185

Internal or External? 187

Term 188

Finances...190

Chapter 15: Interim Integration..................................193

Organization...194

Culture..197

Teams..200

Projects 203

Chapter 16: The SCILL Model© Assessment 208

Sourcing an Interim: A Tool for Clients 208

Validating an Interim Career: A Tool for Interims 214

Future Outlook for Interim Leaders 217

Resources & Notes 219

Foreword

During a career spanning nearly 25 years, I consider myself fortunate to have worked with and appointed some of the leading talent in the field of Interim Leadership. When I started in the 1990's, the pool of freelance senior leaders was almost exclusively grey-haired men in the twilight of their careers. Now we are witnesses to a truly diverse and exciting talent pool, women and men in the prime of their careers. In fact, the gender mix exceeds that of the permanent ranks of executive leaders. The capability and competence these senior leaders bring to the table keeps improving as the landscape of project opportunity increases. Interim Leaders used to be a distress purchase to cover a crisis or a leadership gap. Now the span of projects - from transformation to operational efficiency, leadership to change management, start-up to strategic realignment - provides the kinds of challenges and opportunities Gig Leaders need to thrive.

The market has however struggled for years to define this vibrant community of senior talent that chooses, yes chooses, a career based on temporary contracts. The concept of Interim Leadership remains at odds with what many perceive as the norm. Why would anyone forgo the comfort of the corporate duvet with all its benefits, right? In just under 40 years the idea that a career professional enters the workforce and remains with one company, possibly for life, has been turned on its head.

Born in Holland in the 60's as a result of onerous employment legislation, the concept of Interim Leadership has many names. The Europeans settled on Interim Management as they struggled to disassociate themselves with the established "temp" market place. The exception to the rule (as is so often the case) has been the French, who chose Management de Transition as "interim" is synonymous with lower-level temporary recruitment. In the United States, the market is comfortable with the broad categorization of Consultant, although the term Interim Leadership is emerging in employment vocabulary. Interim Leaders, or Interim Executives, are in fact a distinct and increasingly relevant cadre of professionals. The term, Gig Leader, provides the universal tag for this army of highly competent and immediately accessible senior-level talent.

· ·

There is evidence to suggest that a gig leader can drive through more substantial change and provide a greater return on investment than a permanent employee

· ·

The most significant development over the last decade has been the level of understanding by corporate leaders in all functions of the value and impact that the interim talent pool delivers. In the past, there was suspicion about why an executive was between permanent jobs; today that scenario lacks this stigma so long as the due diligence on the Interim Leader is thorough. There is evidence to suggest that a gig leader can drive through more substantial change and provide a greater return on investment than a permanent employee, as they are fueled by their independence and motivation to deliver within the terms of their engagement.

I remember my first meeting with Neil Grant in 2000 when he was just setting out on his gig career, full of optimism and drive. The industry was still in its pioneering stage and Neil shared the same concerns as most about breaking out on his own for the first time but was determined to make it work. I was keen to help him succeed as an Interim Leader and now we are fortunate that he, together with some other outstanding contributions from professional Gig Leaders, has taken time to put pen to paper. Neil has had a particularly successful career as a Gig Leader, delivering value for 17 clients over 17 years. His expertise as an Interim Leader and his deep insight into this career choice has led to the development of the SCILL model of Interim Leadership described in this book.

With so much of the existence of senior-level executives boiled down to projects, is it a surprise that we seek those who truly understand how to deliver impactful change at pace? Interim Leaders survive off the fact that they are only as good as their last gig, and place enormous energy into each assignment. Gig Leaders, as Neil describes in this book, are nimble, savvy, adept leaders who deliver results. They are decision makers. They must be experts functionally, able to quickly win hearts and minds, assimilate huge amounts of data and cultural cues, while continuing to learn.

The Rise of the Gig Leaders provides a truly contemporary assessment of our industry. Drawing from industry research, case studies, and insights from both Interim Leaders and their clients *Gig Leaders* serves as a "how to" for professionals considering this field for the first time. Just as importantly, it is a "why to" for those executive leaders, clients, and hiring managers seeking greater clarity on where and when to use this potent resource effectively.

NICK ROBESON

Nick Robeson is the former Chairman of the UK Interim Management Association, former CEO of both Hemming Robeson & Alium Partners. Now Managing Partner of Boyden in the United Kingdom, Nick began his career in interim management in 1997, building his reputation by successfully identifying high-caliber interim and permanent C-suite talent for his clients.

Introduction

"Most organizations exploit only a fraction of the knowledge, experience, and intellectual capital that is available to them. But the healthy ones tap into almost all of it."
— Patrick Lencioni, *The Advantage*

An interim leader is one of the most valuable, yet unexploited, resources for building organizational health in the modern era. Diane Mulcahy describes the context for interim leadership in *The Gig Economy*: "Companies are taking previous full-time jobs and breaking them down into smaller projects or tasks to be automated, outsourced, or contracted out. It's cheaper, more flexible, and more efficient to do so." This is the premise for the rise of gig leaders. Gig leaders do more than just fill "jobs", they assume significant leadership roles in growing organizations worldwide.

"People are not your most important asset. The right people are," notes Jim Collins in *Good to Great*. Collins' insight speaks to the importance of choosing the right leadership. *Gig Leaders* provides organizational leaders and strategists with a close look at interim leadership and a model for building a flexible, effective approach to critical-impact leadership in any organization. This leadership option is essential in today's organizations as executives must navigate an age of agility, technology, and choice.

This book also provides a comprehensive look at interim leadership from both an interim's and client's point of view. It explores the compelling reasons a client hires an interim leader and why an executive chooses an interim career; it also provides hands-on examples, testimonials, and case studies across a wide range of industries. What qualities and competencies distinguish an interim leader from a permanent leader, consultant, and other resourcing options? Why is an interim leader especially successful at leading change? What does a client need to consider to ensure the "right fit" when hiring an interim leader? These and other essential questions are addressed through useful tools, such as the SCILL Model© and GREAT competencies. These provide a framework — long requested by senior leaders – for understanding an interim leader's strengths and skills.

Gig Leaders is a useful handbook and resource for business leaders, human resource professionals, and change/project managers. It is divided into sections that stand alone or can be used as a whole. In Part I, clients and interims share their experiences, and the strengths of permanent leaders, interims, and consultants are defined. Part II establishes the framework of the SCILL Model© and presents detailed case studies from varied industries. Part III considers roles and competencies, including coaching and change leadership, that distinguish interim leaders. Part IV delivers tactical "how-to" information, including assessments for both clients and interims, contract tips, and useful resources. My vision for this book is to inform readers about the distinctive contribution of interim leadership since its beginnings in Holland in the 1960s – and its growing relevance around the world today.

During the 1990's, authors Charles Handy and William Bridges predicted changes to the world of work that are especially relevant to the rise of gig leaders. Consider Handy's analogy of a doughnut in *The Empty Raincoat*. The doughnut comprises a central core of key employees and an outside hole comprised of portfolio workers who provide the ultimate in flexibility and effectiveness. In Handy's earlier book, *The Age of Unreason*, he predicted a "shamrock organization, based around a core of essential executives and workers supported by outside contractors and part-time resources." In *Job Shift* William Bridges states, "Work will not be contained in the familiar envelopes we call jobs". He even uses the term "gig" when postulating that "the terms of work have been reframed away from positions and towards assignments or even gigs." These doughnuts, shamrocks, and gigs shape the context for the advent of interim leadership.

Handy and Bridges' vision can be seen today in the rise of the "gig economy". A 2017 report on U.S. employment from Upwork and the Freelancers Union reveals that more than ever, professionals are choosing to freelance; in fact, up to 35% of the total U.S. workforce in 2017 were contract, freelance workers. According to the research paper *The Rise and Nature of Alternative Work Arrangements in the United States, 1995-2015* (March 29th, 2016) published by Lawrence F. Katz and Alan B. Krueger, "94% of net job growth in the past decade was in the alternative work category (non-permanent employment)", and interim leaders are at the cutting edge of this trend in the world of work. In addition, human resource professionals observe a global shift over the last decade in demand for those who perform jobs focused on skills, rather than career paths. This is driven by organizational needs for speed and agility which fuel the increasing requirement to supplement the permanent workforce with other talented professionals. It is much faster, for example, to hire a contract worker than a permanent professional. In addition, new technologies and options for virtual work fuel these shifts in the workforce and the ways organizations and gig workers connect.

In *Accelerate (XLR8)*, John Kotter paints a picture of the world of work: "The world is now changing at a rate at which the basic systems, structures, and cultures built over the past century cannot keep up with the demands being placed on them." He discusses a constant organizational challenge related to this: "You find yourself going back again and again to the same small number of trusted people to lead key initiatives. That puts obvious limits on what can be done and at what speed." One way in which Kotter suggests this challenge can be alleviated is to, "selectively hire people who see and appreciate the true turbulence you face." This is an opportunity for interim leaders.

A 2017 Deloitte Human Capital Trends survey suggests, "As organizations become more digital, they face a growing imperative to redesign themselves to move faster, adapt more quickly, learn rapidly, and embrace dynamic career demands. Leading organizations are moving past the design phase to actively build this new organization." Also, there is the impact of the attitude of millennials towards work that indicates a growing acceptance of the gig economy. Many millennials are confident about virtual employment, intent on making an impact throughout their careers, and eager to find an ideal work-life balance. As the twenty-first century progresses, the traditional working relationship between employer and employee is likely to keep transforming.

Given this cultural and economic context around the world, an interim leader is increasingly relevant to the workplace of today and the future. In *Future Fit*, Giles Hutchins points to one of the main reasons for this: "increasing volatility, complexity and uncertainty is the new norm, hence our organizations need to be able to not just survive but thrive amidst unceasing transformation." This "new norm" requires agile responses, especially in the way organizations consider models of leadership. While permanent leadership provides impact and critical direction, and consultancies provide objective impetus, there is a clear need for temporary experienced leaders to inject gravitas and acceleration at certain moments of organizational development. As Sir Leonard Peach, the ex-Chairman of IBM, reflects in Russell and Daniell's book, *Interim Management, the New Career Choice for Senior Managers*:

> "One good result from the recessions of the early 80s and the early 90s was the recognition that many able people became available on the labor market ... this convinced some employers that they too may gain from individuals with width and variety of experience, rather than depth in one particular company or industry and that, in given situations, the injection of talent and competence for a short term may be more productive than reliance on individuals with long continuous spells of employment."

Reflecting on today's economies and society's norms, it is apparent that more professionals are choosing a portfolio career. The Confederation of British Industry business guide, *Interim Executive Management*, describes interim leadership as, "the management of transition, change, uncertainty or crisis by a 'suitably over-qualified' executive at or near board level, commissioned on an assignment basis." In *Gig Leaders*, the term "interim" describes an experienced (possibly ex C-suite) leader who intentionally chooses to work with organizations for temporary periods of time in essential leadership roles. Clients often ask an interim leader to take on a line role that is vacant –this may involve team leadership responsibilities. An interim differs from a consultant, although the two labels are sometimes used interchangeably, in that he or she is invariably over-qualified for the role, has profound experience of organizational culture, strategy, and operations, and is able to inject pace, precision, and performance with dynamic change outcomes. An interim leader executes organizational strategy - while a consultant delivers ideas and solutions.

· ·

An interim leader is able to inject pace, precision, and performance with dynamic change outcomes.

· ·

My journey as an interim began quite serendipitously when a friend and colleague in the resourcing business asked me, "Have you ever thought of taking a contract instead of another permanent job?"

Looking back, I began my career as a bank clerk when I was 17. I wanted to earn money rather than attend university. I spent 14 years in various organizations in the United Kingdom exploring a career in Information Technology – operations, programming, analysis, and project management. I transitioned from IT to a career in Human Resources via the change-management route. It was a big shift, but absolutely the right one at the time! I decided that professional qualifications and further education were a good thing after all, and in my free time pursued a master's degree and chartered professional status in management and leadership development. After almost a decade of developing my career in leadership development, I was laid off twice in two years. My expectation that the job market would look after someone who was bright enough to commit to an organization was naïve. After the second lay off, I had an answer to this predicament. I was ready for more challenge and wanted to take control of my professional life; I was ready to choose a career as an interim leader.

"I have a client who is looking for a 'big hitter' to design a learning and development strategy for their corporate functions – are you interested?" This was a question asked of me by a recruitment professional. Of course, when this person suggested that I might be a "big hitter", the task of controlling my ego was the biggest challenge. Then he convinced me to reflect on my major achievements of the past decade and my passion for leadership development, and I decided to take the leap.

During this time, I took an assessment test designed to match my personal drivers and strengths with the right career choice. The results suggested that I needed security, relationships, and predictability. Clearly, the prospect of a contract rather than permanent role, was not in keeping with my profile. I thought to myself, "I don't have to be stereotyped by an assessment, I can choose whatever career I want!" Clearly the attitude of someone willing to learn, change, and take control of their destiny!

Since I signed my first contract as an interim leader in late 2001, I have worked around the world across industry sectors as an interim leader. I am now at a vantage point in my career to inform an even wider audience about interim leadership.

Having been based in the United Kingdom for more than 30 years, the term "interim leader" or "interim executive/manager" has long been familiar to me. Now that I am based in the United States, I am happy to say that the demand for interim leaders is increasing and executive opportunities labeled "interim leader" frequently punctuate the job market. Bob Jordan, CEO of the Association of Interim Executives, explains that the "interim leadership market in the U.S. is growing rapidly as the ongoing demands of businesses and nonprofits are matched with the increasingly fungible nature of leadership."

In many ways, interim leadership has gained popularity in the United States and around the world because of the transition Taylor Pearson describes in *The End of Jobs* as, "the shift from the Knowledge economy to the Entrepreneurial economy." An interim leader has the skills, experience, and credentials needed to thrive in a Knowledge economy, but really shines when the imagination and leadership of an entrepreneur is needed. Entrepreneurship, long considered the domain of start-ups, also describes the culture of progressive organizations; these are organizations whose leadership recognizes the need to create innovative products, exploit cutting-edge technology, and develop new markets. An interim has broad and deep knowledge and thrives in such an entrepreneurial market. An interim brings distinctive leadership and expertise to entrepreneurial organizations that seek substantial change and innovative thinking. As a "gig leader" an interim is in many ways an entrepreneur and excels at bringing fresh leadership, energy, and ideas to create lasting change and deliver results.

About the Author

Neil Grant has more than 20 years' experience as a business leader in the fields of leadership, talent, and organizational development. His expertise in building leadership, team, and personal capability as major levers of business strategy and performance, has resulted in clients engaging him across numerous industry sectors around the world. He is frequently asked to lead client projects and deliver significant transformation in Leadership and Organizational Development.

Neil's insight into individual and organizational effectiveness has resulted in lasting changes for organizations. His areas of expertise include:

- Enterprise leadership development frameworks
- Integrated talent management strategies
- Design and delivery of leadership development programs
- Organizational performance and change
- Design of learning architecture and curricula

- Executive coaching

Neil has a master's degree in leadership development from Coventry University (UK), is a chartered graduate member of the Institute of Personnel & Development and has a post-graduate diploma in Coaching & Mentoring Practice from Oxford Brookes University (UK). He publishes a blog, writes articles, and is a leading authority on leadership development and interim leadership. A native of the UK, Neil now lives in the Chicago area with his wife, Irene.

Neil is the owner of Focal Leadership LLC, specializing in leadership development and interim consultancy.

(www.focalleadership.com).

PART I

Today's Interim Leaders

CHAPTER 1

Why Interim Leaders?

"It is not the strongest species that survive, nor the most intelligent, but the ones most able to adapt to change."
— Charles Darwin, *The Origin of Species*

Today's workplace values skilled, independent contractors who work alongside full-time employees. This is an ideal environment for interim leaders as well as specialists and consultants. In fact, Diane Mulcahy's observation about the future of work, described in *The Gig Economy,* is consistent with the world that interim leaders have already discovered. She predicts that by the time today's kids grow up, becoming an employee and getting a full-time job will be the exception, not the rule. Interim leaders embrace this reality and already know that having a diverse portfolio of "good work", as Mulchaly explains it, "will be the new normal, and being a full-time employee for a single employer the exception." This shift to a "gig economy" is a fertile context for "gig leaders"—highly skilled interim leaders.

More than ever, the vacuum of immediately available expert leaders needs to be filled. Employers and leaders must increasingly exercise foresight and agility as they resource their organizations. Mike Johnson observed in the 1998 Economist Intelligence Unit report, "There is a new phenomenon sweeping the global business world: a serious shortage of qualified people to meet the fast-growing needs of corporations." This phenomenon is even more prevalent in today's organizations. This chapter explores the context for choosing an interim leader and why this is a relevant, vital option for today's organizations and leaders.

Why interim leaders? There are several aspects to consider:

- Change: Organizational change shapes the growing need for interim leaders
- Context: Organizational conditions in which an interim leader is a valuable option
- Interim Profile: Common misperceptions about and strengths of an interim leader
- Leadership Options: The difference between an interim and consultant, and the value each adds
- Geographic Perspective on Markets: Geographic perspective on interim leadership, with a look at European and U.S. markets

Changing Organizational Models

Engaging an interim leader is an effective approach to leading and building organizations; it is also a mark of those who embrace change. Consider Charles Handy's insights in *The Second Curve*:

> ". . .to move forward in many areas of life it is sometimes necessary to change radically, to start

a new course that will be different from the existing one, often requiring a whole new way of
looking at familiar problems. Those who have
been in charge of the first curve have to begin to
think differently about the future, or, more often,
let others lead the way up the new curve."

Handy echoes Mulcahy's predictions about the shift to a "gig
economy" when he writes, "I have often wondered why more
individuals with valuable specialist skills do not step outside
the organization, selling their skills or intellectual property back
into the organization instead of giving it away for a salary – it
may only be a matter of time before the contractual organization becomes the norm." An interim leader is at the cutting
edge of this change in the workplace. The conventional world
of work with long-standing organizational job hierarchies and
impregnable leadership cliques is ineffective for competitive organizations in the twenty-first century.

In modern organizations, the paradigm of effective leadership
is not something as simplistic as a stable, long-standing group
of leaders who have been with the organization since college.
Collins and Porras in their 1994 classic, *Built To Last*, suggest
that external hiring and stimulating change are not linked.
While this observation does have legitimacy, it is not an ab-
solute truth. The modern corporate world has changed significantly since the 1990's. With the advance of technology, global
opportunities, and need for agility and reinvention, there is often a need to inject fresh ideas to strategy and common practice
– something that new leaders can stimulate. Collins and Porras
also describe how one of the most important steps a leader can
take to build a visionary company is not an action, but a shift

in perspective. Leaders who are not deeply embedded in the organization can accelerate a shift in perspective. It is commonplace for leaders to be grown or hired into organizations. They develop an affinity with the culture and strategy and set goals to deliver successful outcomes. While Collins and Porras advocate homegrown core leadership, the changing dynamics of organizational development require leaders who can navigate different tiers and areas of expertise.

· ·

Leaders who are not deeply embedded in an organization can accelerate a shift in perspective.

· ·

The world of work is changing. Corporations that have entertained or embraced an interim leader as part of the solution to growth and transformation almost unanimously celebrate this option as a success. Leaders who embrace diverse leadership models and look beyond the wall of familiar solutions will be at the front of the pack. As Giles Hutchins notes in *Future Fit*, "The times in which we live herald paradigmic and metamorphic shifts challenging what we do and the way we do it, calling into question our sense of purpose, and demanding wholly new ways of creating and delivering value."

Why is an interim well positioned to lead in today's organizations?

- An interim learns from multiple experiences how to make things happen
- An interim navigates numerous cultures and leadership styles, developing his or her savvy to lead
- An interim develops a cadence of working, with a diverse portfolio of clients and a wide range of experience,

that allows him or her to bring balance and an informed perspective

- An interim embraces a commitment to change without protecting his or her tenure
- An interim is a rich source of wisdom and expertise

These virtues play strongly in a workplace that appears to be increasingly restless with not repeating the models of the past – not only because of a thirst for change, but a need for relevance.

Leadership Options and the Interim Advantage

An organization seeking an additional leadership resource to tackle specific challenges has several options:

1) Search for a permanent resource (often someone who is already doing this role in another organization) or promote an internal resource
2) Retain a consulting organization and leverage their experience
3) Seek a contractor with a specific skill set
4) Engage an interim to bring expertise, lead, and achieve results

Often senior leaders do not have the luxury of a prolonged timeframe to search for a permanent solution if the organizational need is urgent. Consultancies can offer experience, scale, and intelligence, but typically bring their own overheads and proprietary models that may not be suitable for the organization's specific need. Internal resources may lack the cutting edge or availability that would make the difference to the need in question.

- -

"Company directors with direct experience of interim management believe that interims are a more suitable and cost-effective way to implement change or transition than management consultants – by a ratio of more than 5:1."

- -

What does an interim leader offer? An interim who has worked in the same industry has first-hand knowledge of similar organizational challenges (sometimes on multiple occasions). He or she also demonstrates shrewdness and informed judgement - often being the best resourcing solution. Indeed, a BIE/MORI *Captains of Industry* survey conducted in 2001 states: ". . . company directors with direct experience of interim management believe that interims are a more suitable and cost-effective way to implement change or transition than management consultants – by a ratio of more than 5:1."

Interestingly, one need that unites interim leaders and consultants is to add greater value to client organizations than the clients pay for. Dembitz and Essinger describe this in *Breakthrough Consulting*:

> "Consulting must be more about giving than taking because ultimately it works only if the consultant has a service to offer – one consisting typically of elements such as strategic advice, practical skills, contacts or general inspiration – whose value exceeds what the user is paying for."

One can easily make this argument for an interim leader; when successful, an interim gives more to organizations, people, and projects, than a client might initially have anticipated.

Besondy and Travis suggest in *Leadership On Demand* that an interim can function in strategic or operational capacities, or both, and that the interim's value is "to bridge the performance vacuum between transition events and to avoid the deep declines and valleys common with a full-time employment strategy." While an interim is effective in either a strategic or operational role, the interim's critical contribution is to accelerate, redefine, and deliver organizational change, which might not necessarily be the same as a "bridge". It is important to understand the term "interim" in this context. Interim does not necessarily mean a holding, transitional role between permanent appointments. Indeed, for an interim leader this is rarely the case. The reason an interim leader brings value to an organization has a completely different dimension than to provide cover. An interim is a change agent, dynamic achiever, and motivated fixer!

· ·

An interim is a change agent, dynamic achiever, and motivated fixer.

· ·

When and why do organizations consider hiring an interim leader? Organizations want more flexibility. They want a resourcing model that allows for injections of expertise as well as the stability of leadership to implement long-term strategy. Organizations often consider the option of an interim leader when they need an immediate, highly experienced resource to lead acceleration and transformation. As William Bridges explains in *Job Shift*, "Because conventional jobs inhibit flexibility and speedy response to the threats and opportunities of a rapidly changing market, many organizations are turning over even their most important tasks to temporary and contract workers." Hiring an interim is also a pragmatic choice; it does not disturb the dynamics of organizational hierarchies, progression, and career interests. Everyone knows that the interim is there for a temporary period of time and is not a threat to succession planning.

A strong consequence of hiring an interim is to introduce talent, drive, and delivery into an organization. Having an interim leader on board inspires others to raise their game, provides excellent on-site mentoring, and disturbs any inertia that may exist. "Importing intellectual capital" is how McGovern and Russell, in *A New Brand of Expertise,* describe the opportunity that hiring an interim brings. An interim leader adds gravitas; an interim is a heavyweight resource who can make a significant difference.

Interim Strengths and Misperceptions

The UK-based Interim Management Association defines an interim leader:

- A top-level independent executive or project manager
- An expert in his or her field
- A high-level performer with a track record of quantifiable achievement
- A possessor of drive and energy
- A perceptive individual capable of adapting to new environments and delivering results
- Available immediately

Despite this glowing definition, it often takes first-hand experience, tangible results, or a referral from a reputable source for the client to be convinced of the value of a potential hire. For those who have not experienced the benefits of working with an interim leader, it pays to address common misperceptions —and the strengths an interim leader offers.

INTERIM STRENGTHS	COMMON MISPERCEPTIONS
Interim leaders have often held C-Suite or senior leadership roles in numerous organizations.	Interim leaders fail to hold down a successful permanent role.
Interim leaders have chosen this as a career path; they are not interested in permanent roles.	Interim leaders are just looking for their next permanent role and filling in time with contract work.
Interim leaders are experienced business leaders who deliver and implement solutions.	Interim leaders are merely consultants by another name.

An interim leader engages with the client by having an "interim mindset". This is primarily to exceed the expectations of the client in delivering the assignment, build rapport and stakeholder support, and to do all this with a knowledge that the interim will move on from the organization once this is achieved. This is a goal-oriented mindset. It is not unusual, however, for a client to extend an interim's contract and expand the scope of the interim's contribution once the client has experienced the quality of the interim's work.

An interim leader is more than an intellectually bright individual who develops great solutions; an interim is a leader who is used to leading organizational dynamics at an executive level. Sometimes an interim is hired to tackle tightly-defined projects, and on other occasions an interim is instrumental in defining corporate strategy. Clients should not be surprised if the interim makes broad observations about direction, design, and culture. An interim leader brings an executive perspective, developed during years of experience and application, that renders him or her invaluable.

Interim v. Consultant

What precisely is an interim leader and how is he or she different from other types of leaders or consultants? The illustration below unpacks the primary focus to expect from a permanent

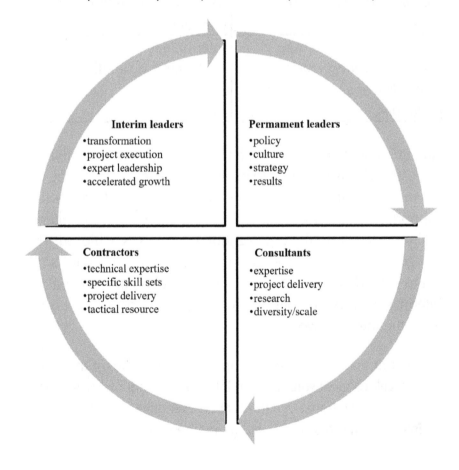

Interim leaders
- transformation
- project execution
- expert leadership
- accelerated growth

Permanent leaders
- policy
- culture
- strategy
- results

Contractors
- technical expertise
- specific skill sets
- project delivery
- tactical resource

Consultants
- expertise
- project delivery
- research
- diversity/scale

leader, interim leader, consultant, and contractor. The definition of what to expect from each is of course highly generic and these accountabilities are often interchangeable. The illustration does however serve as an important introduction to the essential differences between these resources.

Permanent leaders are custodians of the major themes of organizational development, i.e., policy, culture, strategy, and results. The primary reason for considering an interim leader as a resource option is to enhance the permanent leaders' ability to deliver on their custodianship.

· ·

The primary reason for considering an interim leader as a resource option is to enhance the permanent leaders' ability to deliver on their custodianship.

· ·

Consultants, whether they be independent or from a large consulting organization, are at their best when conducting research, designing solutions, and providing scale to support the delivery of organizational change. Interim leaders differ from consultants in that they are experienced business leaders with deep experience of leading change in many organizations. Interims not only provide accelerated thought-leadership and organizational change, but execution – hands-on leadership of that change.

Contractors are often Subject Matter Experts (SME's) who are excellent resources for narrow elements of skill requirements. For example, a contractor might be hired to augment a specific IT or accounting function during a crunch period.

It is especially important to understand the difference between a consultant and an interim, although the lines are blurred. To suggest that an interim leader is a doer, while a consultant is an advisor, is possibly a harsh assessment, but it gets to the core of the hands-on contribution of an interim leader. McGovern and Russell describe the difference in *A New Brand of Expertise*: "A consultant makes recommendations but does not get involved with implementation, while the latter [interim leader] does." The consultant has an advisory relationship with the client's employees; an interim leader often takes line-management responsibility. Of course, many consultancies do work on the implementation of projects, but often have to offer numerous resources to equal the capacity of an interim leader. An interim leader is frequently credited with providing a superior contribution than a consultant, in terms of depth of experience, faster results, and greater commitment.

Geographic Perspective on Markets

The maturity of interim leadership is greatest in Europe; in the United States the market is less mature but growing. This is no surprise given the fact that, as discussed by Nick Robeson in the Foreword, Europe is the birthplace of interim leadership. Indeed, it could be argued that the United Kingdom is the most significant geographic hub for interim leaders. The *Institute of Interim Management Survey 2014* suggests that there are 16,000 interims based in the UK. Many interims who are sourced through agencies based in the UK find themselves engaged with clients around the world. Nick Robeson suggests that any UK organization over £10m p.a. turnover has used interim resources, and the larger the organization, the more interim leaders become a strategic "gig" resource.

The opportunities in the U.S. market merit consideration. While the market is less mature, it is trending upwards. Two leading interim providers, Bill Flannery (Partner, Boyden, Pittsburgh, Pa.) and Bob Jordan (CEO, Association of Interim Executives, Chicago, Il.), share their insights on the U.S. market. Both Flannery and Jordan launched their interim services in about 2000 and expect growth as familiarity with interims increases. Bob Jordan suggests that there could be around 500,000 interim leaders in the U.S., although the understanding of an "interim leader" is still a little vague to accurately validate this number.

1. **How would you describe the interim executive market in the U.S.?**

   Pace of growth:

   Flannery: "The corporate world is not educated about this and the heads of HR aren't familiar with this but are very interested when they find out about it."

   Jordan: "It is growing rapidly and will eventually be mainstream."

   Sector / industry specific:

   Flannery: "There will be demand in manufacturing, because these organizations have legacy issues to deal with and haven't built up their leadership bench strength."

   Jordan: "The demand for interim leaders follows the private equity world – technology, healthcare, manufacturing, business services – not government."

2. **How do you see the future for interim executives?**

> **Flannery:** *"It's a bright future. Most leaders are interested in this as an option. There is a big talent shortage – baby boomers are retiring and there is not a vast leadership bench to step in."*

> **Jordan:** *"Demand is accelerating based on increased awareness."*

Interim leadership is more established in some global regions than others, and is present in both public and private sectors. There are established interim businesses in most main European countries, with the UK, France, and Germany leading the field. Elsewhere this type of leadership is accessed via consultancies rather than established interim agencies, although these are growing in the U.S. and China. The potential in India is enormous although there are currently regulations that obstruct its growth. The Nordics and Russia are emerging markets.

Consider the following statistics about the UK interim market from the *Institute of Interim Management Survey 2014:*

- Average age of an interim leader is 52
- 72:28 male to female
- Top five most common roles; CEO/MD/General Manager, Director, Head of Function, Project Manager, Consultant
- 64% of interim leaders work in the private sector
- 71% of interim leaders are on assignment at any point in time
- 52% of assignments focus on change or transformation
- Interims average 167 billed days per year
- 80% of interims are sourced for assignments by clients

and agencies rather than seeking assignments

As the world of work changes, the need for interim leaders is growing. "We're at a unique moment in human history where power is dispersing from organizations to individuals," notes Taylor Pearson in *The End of Jobs*. This insight, together with sound research and the voices of business leaders, clients, and interim leaders, adds weight to the argument for interim leaders. As the positive impact of interim leaders becomes more evident, and the familiarity with interim leadership grows, business leaders will look increasingly at these professional leaders as a significant resource to build their organizations.

CHAPTER 2

What Clients Say

"People who learn to master more volatile career paths also usually become more comfortable with change generally and thus better able to play more useful roles in organizational transformations."

— John Kotter, *Leading Change*

Clients who choose to hire an interim leader have specific reasons for doing so and are often highly satisfied with the results of the interim's contribution. An interim's impact is often crucial for the host organization. If this is the case, then why aren't interim leaders more widely used? This elephant in the room needs addressing. The Confederation of British Industry suggest, in their business guide *Interim Executive Management,* that many companies simply don't consider interim management as an alternative –they remain rooted in their old ways, partly due to a lack of understanding about the interim concept. According to UK research, published in September 2000 by Sambrook Research in association with the Institute of Management Consultancy, 92% of companies that used interims would "probably/definitely" use them again. The Confederation of British Industry goes on to note, ". . . the interim route brings immediate extra horsepower to the organization and injects objectivity and fresh ideas based on real 'hands-on' experience."

In this chapter, clients share the reasons they elected to bring an interim leader into their organizations to fulfill specific needs. Each client's testimonial is followed by an analysis of the essential qualities of interim leadership addressed by the specific assignment. Each example illustrates the reasons why an interim is the "resource of choice" for certain organizational needs.

Why do clients choose to hire an interim leader? There are many reasons:

- Critical business need
- Leadership of organizations and people
- Change management
- Focus that is free of organizational politics
- External expertise
- Excellent, measurable results
- Immediate course correction
- In-depth subject matter experience
- Independent, objective perspective
- Thought leadership respected at senior levels
- Ability to quickly assimilate and disengage
- Pace of delivery
- Cost-effective to hire a single leadership resource as opposed to several

Assuming that clients have been exposed to the concept of interim leadership, their rationale for hiring an interim provides further insight to their specific organizational need. The varied client scenarios below illustrate the reasons why, in each case, hiring an interim was the right choice.

Client 1: Director of Leadership Development, Professional Services Corporation.

Revenue $1.65bn. Employees 8,000.

As we evolve towards a "gig economy", longer-term consultant relationships are going to be a part of that picture. Granted, they may look different depending on the precise business need, but the general idea –sourcing external expertise to meet a well-defined remit—makes sense. All too often today, internal re-sources are already "over-clocked" with more demands of their time than they are already capable of handling well. When we brought a long-term consultant onto our team, we were seek-ing to acquire external expertise to focus on a specific business need for a multi-year initiative. This resource became a team member in many respects like any other employee –with one exception: they maintained a clear focus on a single area for which they clearly had the skillset. This allowed us to meet sig-nificant milestones we might otherwise have never met or met with quality issues.

This client's experience points to several critical reasons for hir-ing an interim:

- External expertise: the client identifies an interim who has a track-record and experience in a specific skill-set and professional discipline. The client ring fences a scope of work most effectively met by hiring expertise quickly.
- Focus: The client connects an interim with a specific ob-jective, and removes the distractions of other organiza-tional activities to enable the interim to deliver critical objectives.

- <u>Business need:</u> As business needs become pressing and increasingly integrated for organizational success, an interim is able to address these needs with a coherent and business-aware capability.
- <u>Meeting significant milestones:</u> Often organizations are moving at such a pace that significant milestones are dependent on resources that are spread thinly across multiple activities. These milestones are critical for ongoing organizational development; an experienced interim is able to deliver them.
- <u>Quality:</u> An interim has built a reputation for excellence and achievement. This provides deep reassurance to client organizations that rely on quality resources to deliver key projects.

This client weighed the options for delivering a significant business requirement and decided that an interim was the best solution. Clearly, the requirement was a project that once delivered, did not require continuity of employment. Yet the client needed to minimize the risks for its delivery by bringing an interim leader's deep expertise into the organization for the duration of the project.

Client 2: Chief Learning Officer, Outsourced Service Provider.

Revenue £3.1bn. 50,000 employees.

Hiring interims to just fill a gap, do more of the same, is easy and perhaps a bit lazy. I want an interim to create change at what I call "turning points". This can come about opportunistically because someone has left a key role, but more often it will be a planned intervention. Using an interim to help the business turn a corner or grab a new challenge plays to his or her temperament and strengths. It also means you don't have to retain change-junkies permanently in business-as-usual roles in the hope that their day will come.

What is fascinating about client rationales for hiring an interim is that different critical drivers appear prominently in each client's testimonial. For example, for the client above, the following critical drivers are apparent:

- <u>Change catalyst:</u> The client's phrases — "turning points", "turn a corner", "grab a new challenge" —describe what is home field for an interim. An interim thrives on delivering change and addressing business opportunities that require proactive transformational thinking.
- <u>Connects and disconnects effectively:</u> This client's needs play to the temperament and strengths of an interim leader. An interim has certain values and behaviors that attract these sorts of assignments. An interim connects quickly, delivers effectively, and disconnects positively.
- <u>Apolitical:</u> An interim is objective, rather than being a political animal, career-ladder climber, or security seeker.

Clients looking for a catalyst to accelerate change often find that an interim leader provides just that. And the interim does this without any baggage; an interim is an expert in his or her field who understands organizations, delivers critical projects, and works at a pace that is undistracted by other organizational clutter.

Client 3: Global Learning Director, Consumer Goods Company.

Turnover €52.7bn. Employees 169,000

There are some clear and distinct advantages to appointing an interim leader into a leadership position. In particular, when there are situations when we urgently need to "steady the ship" an experienced hand is required to bring instant stability and credibility to our operations. The combination of instant competence, experience, and dispassionate objectivity are essential ingredients in chaotic, uncertain, and unpredictable times. Long term, I'd almost always prefer to appoint a homegrown talent to leadership roles, yet often the short-term appointment of an interim buys time so we're not rushing decisions, can prepare our succession completely, and also provide additional mentoring and coaching to the talent in-situ. The apparent disadvantages of not knowing the organization are outweighed by the ability of a good interim to take the tiller quickly and provide an instant course correction. Being an outsider and not a permanent appointment, an interim is more able to avoid the rocks and whirlpools of insidious organizational politics or cultural characteristics.

What are the critical reasons behind this client's choice to hire an interim?

- Urgency: The client needs to hire the best resources to meet a critical organizational project or leadership role; this is not an easy or fast activity. The client needs to retain the services of an expert who is immediately available. This is a great advantage of going down the interim route.
- Credibility / instant competence: An interim often makes an immediate impact. The interim's experience and savvy mean that he or she is instantly recognized as a source of wisdom and gravitas.
- Mentoring and coaching: An interim is often motivated

to pass on the benefits of his or her expertise to others. An interim eagerly adopts the leadership role of building and growing the capability of in-house employees.

- Instant course correction: Fast and impactful contributions characterize the tenure of an interim. The interim brings insight, courageous observations, and dispassionate recommendations.

By acknowledging the advantages of hiring an interim, this client also points to ancillary benefits. An interim leader provides a foil for internal resources that are often impacted by organizational distractions. The interim gives the organization breathing space as its leadership weighs long-term resource planning. An interim provides a relevant, respected, and resilient addition to leadership when an organization acknowledges that to succeed, it must deliver on strategic change.

Client 4: Head of Organizational Development & Talent, Energy Company.

Revenue £28 bn. Employees 30,000.

I hired an interim as I needed someone experienced to hit the ground running with an open mind, without the constraints of internal organizational politics. Interims offer [clients] the opportunity to experiment with a role before committing. They are less precious about what they do and are output focused as they are dependent on recommendations. Interims also arrive without the baggage of some consultancies keen to sell their methodology and create dependency.

This client's observations accurately make the case for hiring an interim:

- <u>Hit the ground running:</u> An interim does not need a long runway before he or she adds value. An interim's experience, insight, and judgment mean he or she makes a difference within hours of starting the assignment. There is a balance of listening and learning before making conclusive observations and a good interim is able to do this effectively.

- <u>Without the constraints of internal organizational politics:</u> Organizations sometimes find themselves paralyzed because they are constrained by leaders who are protecting fiefdoms or are unable to see the possibilities of re-drawing process or systems. An interim brings unconstrained contributions without any baggage. An interim also carries significant gravitas; an interim's proposals are received with authority even if the proposals challenge internal political positioning.

- <u>Experiment with a role before committing:</u> When an organization weighs options regarding leadership positions before making a permanent decision, hiring an interim can provide time and perspective to consider this. It may be that a previous organizational structure has given cause for concern. Hiring an interim who can plug the gap, as well as recommend alternatives, is a pragmatic way forward.

- <u>They are less precious about what they do:</u> While this may be the case for some interims, many would not agree with this client assessment. It may, however, be true that an interim's adaptability means he or she welcomes varied assignments spanning the interim's wide range of capability.

- <u>Without the baggage of some consultancies:</u> This is an important differentiator between interims and consultants, as discussed in Chapter 1 (Why Interim Leaders?). An interim may recommend methodologies and models, but an interim rarely has proprietary rights that will make a client dependent on him or her going forward.

- <u>Output focused and dependent on recommendations:</u> An interim's reputation is characterized by and built on the projects he or she has conquered, and the client relationships cultivated.

Clearly, this client observed that the independence and fresh insight that an interim offers, are major reasons for hiring one.

Client 5: Chief Human Resource Officer, Waste Management Company.

Revenue £614m. 3,500 employees.

The choice to use an interim was not a difficult one to make. The challenge for my client was to accelerate the capabilities of the leadership team as they introduced a new operating model. The interim appointed was a strong professional, not just with the right tools available, but the experience and gravitas to gain the confidence of the CEO and his team. This meant the program of work was delivered effectively and on time.

This client's rationale is consistent with that of others who hire an interim because of the interim's professional credibility, experience, and gravitas.

- <u>Professional credibility:</u> This client's observation "to gain the confidence of the CEO and his team" should not be underestimated. There are many reasons why senior leadership need instant confidence in someone hired to accelerate the capabilities of the broader leadership team. They need to know that the interim can assimilate quickly what the challenge is, rise to the occasion of providing solutions, and speak with insight and boldness about the client's business.

- Trusted by peers: Most interims are confident interacting with senior leadership and speak candidly to senior leaders as peers, rather than as exalted leaders whom they need to impress. This quickly endears an interim to client leaders as a partner, trusted advisor, and source of wisdom.

Client 6: Chief Learning Officer, Energy Company.

Revenue $5.23bn. Employees 6,000.

I've found immense value in leveraging outside thought leadership to help supplement strategic priorities related to leader development and talent management. An interim leader and executive consultant brought a perspective that did not exist internally, and our organization benefitted from his wealth of experience and his ability to connect dots we didn't know existed. Our efforts resulted in a more efficient use of resources and stronger outcomes of leader development planning.

- Thought leadership: A fresh, experienced perspective is a critical reason for hiring an interim. If a client is looking for a value-added resource to help move the organization forward, this is what an experienced interim brings.
- Breadth and depth of knowledge: As the client above points out, the ability to "connect the dots" is a virtue of interim leadership. An interim knows his or her way around organizations and the subject matter of projects.

An interim makes broad and deep connections with other parts of organizational operations and brings strong cohesion to his or her work and that of others. Delivering an outcome of efficiency and strength are a credit to the impact of an interim leader.

Clearly, as these clients observe, hiring an interim leader brings significant acceleration to an organization going through change. The critical reasons that clients cite for hiring an interim leader reveal the distinctive strengths that an interim brings to organizations; an interim delivers specific results and effectively leads people, projects, and change.

CHAPTER 3

What Interims Say

"Taking stock of your real self starts with an inventory of your talents and passions – the person you actually are as a leader."

— Daniel Goleman, *Emotional Intelligence*

Leaders embarking on interim careers need to make a conscious transition from dependence to independence. In *Portfolio Life* David Corbett aptly notes: "Having a self-employed attitude means knowing yourself and believing, thinking, and acting independently. Determine what it is you deeply want to do and go out and create a demand for it." Interim leaders must have a strong personal conviction about their capability and potential contributions, and charisma to make their careers successful.

In this chapter, interim leaders share the reasons they chose this career path. Understanding what motivates an interim is particularly important for clients when selecting an interim for a specific assignment, and for leaders who may be considering interim leadership as a career choice. See Chapter 16 (The SCILL Model© Assessment) for detailed insights and tips on making these choices.

What motivates a senior leader or executive to choose an interim career? The reasons are diverse:

- Desire for variety, challenge, and opportunity
- Changing economic and employment options
- Dissatisfaction with the traditional workplace
- Drive to lead change and be at the cutting edge
- Opportunity to use expertise and skills to fullest potential
- A conscious career shift following being laid off
- Work/ life balance with flexibility to schedule breaks between assignments
- Satisfaction of being in control of what one does and for whom
- Results and purpose-driven leadership style
- Desire for meaningful connection and impact

Shifting Mindsets

William Bridges, looking ahead to the twenty-first century *in Jobshift,* predicted that today's workers need to "forget jobs completely and look instead for work that needs doing – and then set themselves up as the best way to get that work done." In 1994, this was indeed a radical view of the future; today, interim leaders are at the front of the pack in this new world of work. Bridges' prophecy hasn't accelerated as fast as he may have predicted, but the growth of temporary jobs in the workplace is a definite trend. His observation that everyone is a contingent worker led Bridges to suggest that workers need to "develop a mindset, an approach to work, and a way of managing their own careers that is more like that of an external vendor than a traditional employee. Workers will be wise to think that they are 'in business for themselves.'" This applies not only to professionals and technicians, but also to leaders; interims in particular must make this transformation. A Bridges notes, "employees need to consider what it will be like to let go of the whole cluster of attitudes, expectations, assumptions, self-images, and values that went with the idea of 'having a job.'" This is a journey that most interims have traveled to reach a new mindset.

· ·

"Active creators, builders, and architects of their own career trajectories, not the recipients of them."
Diane Mulcahy, *The Gig Economy*

· ·

In *The Gig Economy* Diane Mulcahy describes those who succeed in today's workplace as shifting from "an Employee Mindset to an Opportunity Mindset." This is a shift that interims embrace as they actively carve out their careers. Mulcahy describes how workers with Opportunity Mindsets "see themselves as active creators, builders, and architects of their own career trajectories, not the recipients of them. They accept and expect to generate their own customized version of security, stability, and identity that is separate from any one company or organization. They create their own visions of success and work to achieve it."

Another perspective on the shifting mindset towards work and what motivates an interim leader is discussed by David Corbett in *The Portfolio Life*. Corbett paints a picture of mature workers who, "create a balance of work, learning, leisure, family time, giving back, etc." Certainly, as a career choice, being an interim leader dovetails with Corbett's view of, "working in the form you want." However, his focus on this as a retirement option, is not how an interim sees his or her role. An Interim leader has an Opportunity Mindset. An interim is looking less to create personal balance—although an interim career offers this —but rather to align work opportunities and organizational challenges with personal and professional strengths.

Perhaps above all, the desire to be effective lies at the core of an interim leader's motivation. As Peter Drucker notes in *The Effective Executive*, "Effectiveness is a habit."

What do interims say about their career choice? Of note is the "win-win" correlation between the opportunities interims seek professionally and the organizational challenges that lead clients to hire interims.

Interim Testimonials

Interim 1: Growth and fulfillment

After nine years in the same company I left the security of a well-paid position with all the perks to make the leap to a world where there was no guarantee of success. On reflection, my drivers included:

- *Personal growth: I'd reached a plateau with my previous company where there was little opportunity for me to develop further. After years of thinking about setting up on my own I took the leap.*
- *Flexibility: I wanted the flexibility to work with who I wanted, when I wanted, and where I wanted across multiple sectors and industries.*
- *Reward: there are definite financial rewards to working for yourself; in addition, there is a wealth of reward in supporting different organizations in reaching their*

strategic objectives. The diversity of each contract is highly rewarding to me personally.

As the interim leader above describes, choosing an interim career carries some risk. Equally important there are drivers associated with an interim's optimism, challenge, and achievement-orientation. There is a foundation of self-belief and confidence that drives an interim forward. An interim believes he or she can be successful, add value, and build a future that is personally and professionally fulfilling.

Interim 2: Expertise is valued

It's been a while since I "took the plunge" to be an interim. I have thoroughly enjoyed making the move. I was frustrated in my corporate role, recognising what needed to happen but not getting my voice heard. Suddenly becoming independent, clients started to really listen to what I had to say and take action. As someone who has always thrived amidst change rather than business-as-usual, this has suited me well. Not having to get embroiled in the organization's politics is also a real plus point.

The context of "change" is a recurring theme throughout this book. For an interim, the opportunities and challenges that come with change are central to his or her motivation. As the interim above describes, an interim possesses a strong drive to be acknowledged as an expert. An interim is nimble, learns fast, studies continuously, and tests the boundaries of the status quo – this makes an interim leader an effective, stimulating addition to the leadership of any organization.

Interim 3: <u>Mission-critical challenges</u>

Within 24 hours of my decision to leave permanent employ-ment, a phone call brought news of a project at a senior level in a large listed company which offered career development and a serious challenge. So it has continued for many years, with few signs of candidate bias. The project goes to the candidate with the skills most suited to the role who is available to start immediately. The work is usually "mission critical"—essential for the business, a priority; something needs to change, and the need is now! Contracts are flexible, so resources come as re-quired and leave when projects are completed. A track record of success brings opportunities to repeat as well. An interim has challenge, flexibility, opportunity, career development breadth and depth, and the freedom to plan work and leisure periods. The downside is that these leisure periods may occasionally be longer than desired!

Mission-critical projects are beacons that draw an interim to client organizations. They are also major reasons why these organizations lean on an interim leader as the most effective resource to steer the ship. Chapter 6 (Critical) explores in de-tail the "mission critical" reasons why an interim is so effec-tive. The interim above thrives on meeting critical challenges, despite any gaps in contracts. Contracts, by their very nature, require an interim leader to deal with beginnings and endings in a frequent and effective manner. (Contract tips are presented in Chapter 14).

Interim 4: <u>Influence decision-making at highest levels</u>

I worked in a number of large companies and never made it to chief executive of a large PLC after a number of attempts. I made it to board level, but not to the top where I could influence the direction of the company. Then I did some naval gazing and started to think about what I was good at and enjoyed. I concluded that I liked looking at problems and coming up with novel, radical, and simple solutions to complex problems. I looked at consultancy, but this was back to corporate life; I concluded that being an interim was the right solution. Each time I have an assignment the client wants me to go permanent; I have decided to stick to my ideology and develop an interim career. I have been an interim for 12 years and for each assignment I look for a different function or sector to bring variety to the role.

This interim describes a need to be able to influence decisions and a need for significance. An interim wants to make a difference, be seen and heard, and to play a big role. This doesn't come from a conceited or arrogant perspective, rather it stems from a self-belief and conviction that an interim is a mover and shaker who proves time and again that he or she is successful in many interim roles.

Taking responsibility for one's career direction characterizes the journey of an interim perhaps more so than any other employee or consultant. An interim leader positions him or herself for assignments, develops expertise, and draws energy from the commitment to maintain this career direction rather than be distracted by an alternative.

Interim 5: <u>Adding real value</u>

After 30 years of working in full-time roles, I knew it was time for a change. I came to realize that I am happiest when I can add real value and make a tangible impact on a business. I love troubleshooting, working out what is wrong and finding a solution to fix it. Interim roles provide the perfect outlet for this. Without the politics of full-time positions, which can be frustrating, interim roles are often clear-cut. They generally have set responsibilities, a defined remit, and specific objectives to achieve. As an outsider looking in, you have the benefit of bringing an objective view, with no agenda, and yet can provide advice. Sometimes it might not be what clients wants to hear, but almost certainly it is what they need.

An interim is motivated to make things happen and this interim is no exception. An interim values real results and the ability to bring objectivity—a detached but critical perspective—and has the courage to confront clients with reality. These characteristics are explored further in later chapters, but it is worthy of note that an interim is not a shrinking violet; an interim is a confident, insightful, and often outspoken professional.

Interim 6: Diverse and challenging roles

My interim career started by accident during an interview for a permanent job. After five minutes of not being able to fully answer the interviewer's questions, I stopped the interview and asked if I could simply spend a few minutes explaining how I thought my experience could help them tackle their systems-upgrade issues in a cost-effective manner. I was offered a contract role on the spot. Now, some 20 years and more than 20 assignments later, I still enjoy diverse and challenging roles, where I can add significant "bottom-line" financial value, without the constraints of office politics. I'm still glad to this day that I stopped that interview!

This interim describes the essence of interim leadership: adding significant value without organizational constraints. An interim knows where to plug in most effectively without the overhead of an organizational career. An interim leader seeks meaningful connection and impact. The organization benefits, the interim benefits, and all those connected with the interim and the organization benefit.

"Interim Management is not working temporarily at one job while you are waiting for the next 'proper' job to come along — it is a career choice," note McGovern and Russell in *A New Brand of Expertise*. To be an effective interim, they explain, requires an independence of thought and action that is different from that of a permanent employee who is concerned about keeping his or her job. McGovern and Russell's observations further reinforce the reasons why an interim decides to pursue this mode of working.

PART II

The DNA of Interim Leaders

CHAPTER 4

The SCILL Model©

In *A New Brand of Expertise* McGovern and Russell describe what an interim leader brings to an organization:

> "A hands-on manager: the sort of person who can walk into a situation, rapidly identify what needs to be done, put together a plan and implement it within a given timescale and budget. These managers have the capacity to overcome unseen obstacles, lift the morale of staff, and sort out internal processes and other day-to-day issues along the way. They are also prepared to walk away without any fuss when the job is completed – and even be prepared to recruit his or her successor."

The SCILL Model© is highly consistent with this description and goes even deeper – it defines the DNA of an interim leader. Building on a decades-long career as an interim leader, the author identifies essential qualities that distinguish interim leadership. This is a useful tool for the many corporate leaders who continue to request such a framework, a straightforward way to grasp the concept of interim leadership and distinguish it from other leadership options.

After many years as an interim leader for organizations around the world, learning from interim providers, clients, and other interim leaders, the author developed the SCILL Model© to clearly explain the interim leader role. The five SCILL attributes of interim leadership are:

⟨◎⟩ Focal Leadership LLC

The next five chapters examine each of the SCILL Model© attributes in depth and include "hands-on" case studies.

- *Savvy* – organizational, relational, and cultural
- *Critical* – crisis or turnarounds, growth, integration following a merger or acquisition, cost reduction and value creation, and raising the bar on performance and quality
- *Impact* – dynamic, insightful, results-focused, and courageous
- *Leadership* – personal, situational, transformational, inspirational, and reputational
- *Legacy* – organizations, projects, and people

Case studies for each SCILL attribute illustrate how an interim leader meets specific challenges and adds value to organizations; each case study highlights a specific SCILL attribute in a "real world" business context.

The case studies illustrate:

- <u>Client context</u>: the organizational industry, geography, size, and scope in which the interim leader was asked to deliver their assignment
- <u>Assignment:</u> the specific project the interim leader was asked to deliver
- <u>Results:</u> the outcomes achieved during the project
- <u>Benefits of an interim solution:</u> the reasons why an interim leader was the optimum resource to deliver the results of the assignment

The case study below is a starting point for the discussion of the SCILL Model© attributes presented in Chapters 5-9. An interim leader is often asked to deliver specific projects as well as lead parts of the organization through periods of change. This case study demonstrates how an interim leader transforms teams and impacts an organization, both in the immediate future and the long term.

Case Study: Create Brand Strategy

1. Client Context

<u>Major fast-moving consumer goods player</u> in the UK within the branded foods market, and part of a much larger multinational food and ingredients business with operations across 50 countries. Annual revenue £160m. Number of employees 680.

2. Assignment

<u>Interim Head of Brand</u> for the brand leader within the ethnic foods market reporting to the Marketing Director. A five-month assignment with these key objectives:

- To define and spread best practice for brand strategy and marketing planning across the whole of the UK Marketing and Insights team, covering all brands within the portfolio
- As part of the above, to quickly deliver a brand strategy and marketing plan for the ethnic food brand
- To build a strong and high performing marketing team for this ethnic food brand, to ensure the successful delivery of the brand strategy and marketing plans

3. Results

- Best practice for brand strategy and marketing planning was embedded in the business through a two-stage workshop process. All of the marketing plans for the following financial year followed this new process and the templates provided.
  - o This in turn provided the Marketing Director with a clear and consistent approach across all brands, enabling prioritization and investment decisions across all brands in the portfolio to be taken with full visibility.

- The brand strategy and marketing plan for the ethnic food brand was clearly defined as part of the above process.
  - o This piece of work defined the brand proposition, the business and marketing objectives, and the key challenges and marketing initiatives required to deliver them.
- The immediate marketing team of six was very new, with half of the team only having joined the business in the previous four weeks.
  - o The credibility of the team within the business was low, particularly with the sales team, and this was due in part to a period of under-resourcing for the team and a history of missed deadlines.
  - o Weekly team meetings defined the purpose, key challenges, and how the team needed to operate, as well as providing the sharing of ongoing feedback from other teams in the business.
  - o Planning meeting with the wider sales team resulted in sharing and alignment of the objectives, deliverables, and timescales for respective teams.

The Marketing Director's feedback at the end of the assignment:
- The team had changed from the worst performing team within the business to the best performing team;
- The best practice work on brand strategy and marketing planning had created a step change in how the wider Marketing and Insights department worked as a whole.

4. **Benefits of an Interim Solution**
   - Ability to hit the ground running
     - o The interim's ability to quickly assess organizations and people and to drive constructive change; this

has been significantly enhanced by the fact that the interim has worked across a wide variety of businesses, cultures, and industries.

- Technical expertise
  - o The interim's knowledge of the best practices of brand strategy and marketing planning processes.
- Personal credibility
  - o The interim's ability to build strong working relationships with the immediate team, including senior level leaders and across the wider business, enabled the interim to quickly drive change and take leaders and teams along.

CHAPTER 5

Savvy

Savvy - shrewdness and practical knowledge; the ability to make good judgments

Originating from the Latin word *sapere,* meaning to be wise, "savvy" is the most significant distinguishing attribute of an interim leader. An interim "gets" organizations, relationships, and culture. An interim leader is experienced, smart, and sharp.

. . . .
An interim "gets" organizations, relationships, and culture.
. . . .

David Maister describes a critical stage of trust creation between a client and advisor in *The Trusted Advisor* as, "framing the issue . . . . Framing is the art of crystallizing and encapsulating the client's complex issues (and emotions) into a problem definition that, in an objective manner, provides both insight and a fresh way of thinking about the problem." This ability is at the core of an interim leader's savviness when engaging with projects and clients. Another way of describing savvy in this context is "acumen". The Confederation of British Industry's business guide, *Interim Executive Management,* notes, "Interim leaders bring a wealth of experience and business acumen that help to set a company on the right course for the future."

In what contexts do interim leaders excel in demonstrating their savvy?

- Organizational
- Relational
- Cultural

Organizational Savvy

Whenever an interim engages with a new client, it is imperative that he or she quickly absorbs, understands, and appreciates the organization before the details of the assignment. Most smart professionals conduct research into a future employer before interviewing for a position or beginning employment. For an interim, this practice is essential. When commencing a relationship with a client, an interim needs a solid understanding of the environment they are entering. It is vital that the interim frames an understanding of the "ask" (the contract scope) in the context of the organization.

Organizations are complex and unique. They can be incredibly mature and have existed for more than 100 years, maybe metamorphosing on many occasions. Or they can be vibrant start-ups. Of course, there are variations in between. Ronald Heifetz, Marty Linsky and Alexander Grashow discuss the subtleties of organizations in *The Practice of Adaptive Leadership*: "To identify adaptive challenges confronting an organization, look beyond what people are saying about them. Listen to the song beneath the words." Whatever the organization, the challenges faced in growth, transformation, and stabilization need to be understood in context for an interim intervention to be successful.

To suggest that the same solutions can be "prepackaged" and rolled out to successive organizations when the interim moves between them is naïve. Intellectual property may well be an asset for an interim, but its application is not necessarily homogeneous. As Sir Leonard Peach, ex-Chairman of IBM, reflects in Russell and Daniell's book, *Interim Management*:

> "Interims must have confidence in themselves and their abilities, they must continue to upgrade their competencies and their skills, they must develop their analytical and diagnostic skills recognizing that every situation has unique elements, and the solution for the current customer is not necessarily the same as that which they employed in a previous situation."

Conversations with the client, from the first engagement, need to demonstrate the interim's competence and gravitas, his or her understanding of the client's organization and the broader industry. Many authorities on interim leader skills often cite "listening" as critical to the success of an interim.

An asset management company CEO's ask is an example of why an interim needs to quickly understand the client context for a project. The CEO asked, "I want to align every employee behind a single company culture and ensure that everyone has personal objectives that align to the corporate goals. How can you help me?" Questions like this should not only inspire an interim but offer a challenge. A waffled answer to such a question immediately undermines credibility. The interim's ability to articulate a response with curiosity about the client's company, the motivation for the ask, the challenges, the culture, and the desired outcomes, while providing commentary on the value of aligned culture and goals, is likely to convince the client of the interim's credentials. Asking follow-up questions and engaging the commitment of the CEO and the senior leadership team in delivering the challenge are also essential ingredients in the conversation. Lastly, it is important for an interim to indicate how he or she might tackle such a challenge. This gives the client an idea of the interim's experience, style, and approach.

Acquiring organizational savvy is a prerequisite for any client engagement. There is a wealth of information on the client's organization available in the public domain. An interim should ask a client questions in advance of key conversations with senior leaders. There may even be an agency involved that can be drilled for answers to questions about the client's organization and challenges. Above all, a client must have confidence that a prospective interim understands their industry, the organization, and the specific challenge being discussed. The interim must be able to conduct a conversation that demonstrates this. At an industry and organizational level, an interim could do worse than to conduct a tried and tested PESTLE analysis (political, economic, social, technological, legal, and environmental) on the client's organization, prior to any detailed engagement.

There are several ways to demonstrate organizational savvy:

- Reveal and reflect knowledge of the organizational context during conversations
- Offer insights based on PESTLE analysis
- Be curious, ask great questions that demonstrate an understanding of the organization and the broader industry challenges
- Use examples of other organizations and similar challenges / solutions
- Explore organizational dynamics and structures that might reveal more about the challenges
- Inquire about work already done to address the challenges and prioritization of issues

Essentially, an interim needs to bring a level of experience and insight to convince the client that he or she is not only capable of tackling the challenge but is already motivated to add value. This is done by demonstrating a strong connection with the challenge. As for how much the interim needs to have ready-reckoned solutions for the client, Alasdair Drysdale suggests in *The Interim Director*, "You should think of an interim job as an 80-20. You need to have 80% of the required experience at the outset, and the 20% which you pick up as you go along is a bonus, and a step-up to being able to handle something more demanding in the future." Often, an interim needs to show his or her grasp of the organizational challenge and ability to successfully deliver results in a quick timeframe —within days or weeks, certainly not months. The pace of interim interventions is explored in greater depth in Chapter 7 (Impact).

Being "smart" does not imply that an interim leader always has the answer or the solution. In fact, some of the smartest leaders reserve judgment until they understand the organization and the challenge. It is ineffective for an interim to approach a project by offering a solution, drawing a conclusion, or recommending a methodology before understanding the organizational challenge. Clients know their business and the challenges they are facing. Any prospective solution to their needs requires an interim to have the intelligence, humility, and curiosity to seek a clear understanding before suggesting solutions and next strategies.

· ·

An interim absorbs organizational context, understands the challenge, and offers perspective without the clutter of employment or proprietary baggage.

· ·

An interim absorbs organizational context, understands the challenge, and offers perspective without the clutter of employment or proprietary baggage. Demonstrating organizational savvy is an essential first step for an interim seeking to establish credibility.

Relational Savvy

Relational savvy — the ability to connect with the right stakeholders in the right way with the right intentions —is an essential quality of a successful interim. As Richard Lindenmuth says in *The Outside the Box Executive*, "You must develop the trust of those who sit across the table from you in order to take them where they want to go." David Maister talks about this essential skill in *The Trusted Advisor*: "You don't get the chance to employ advisory skills until you get someone to trust you enough to share their problems with you." Relational savvy is critical in leadership, and perhaps even more so for an interim leader. Timescales are often short, and the stakeholder network is complex. Navigating relationships with skill, sensitivity, and selectivity, is a critical capability.

For an interim, a big piece of the success equation is how likeable he or she is. Can an interim connect emotionally as well as intellectually? Demonstrating a collaborative, engaging, and curious mindset is a great way to build a rapport that leads to trust. If a client does not "connect" with an interim when evaluating him or her as a potential partner to tackle a business challenge, then the prospect of contractually engaging with the interim might be inconceivable. If an interim, for example, comes across as arrogant, cold, or overly-technical, then the likelihood of building relationships and delivering results may be too high a risk from the client's point of view to move forward.

When engaged by a client, assessing the relative value of relationships is critical for an interim. Falling back on familiar models like RACI charts (Responsible, Accountable, Consult, Inform) is a sound approach to building a stakeholder map. This establishes where the power lies, the significance of stakeholder relationships, and where to invest time.

One of the biggest mistakes an interim leader—or any leader for that matter —can make is to focus his or her professional energy on delivering outcomes and not invest equal or more time building relationships and managing stakeholders. An interim trying hard to impress colleagues with his or her ability to tackle a challenge while sidelining the individuals who know the challenge best, who are impacted the most, or who will ultimately sign-off on any proposal, is less than savvy. Investing in relationship building, asking questions, sharing early ideas, conducting research, and keeping key stakeholders informed of progress are all essential elements to delivering high-impact results as an interim.

Sometimes an interim is called on to lead a team of employed staff. There are likely several factors at play:

- The interim is bridging a gap before the appointment of a permanent leader
- The client needs a team to deliver the challenge.
- An interim is needed in addition to consultants, contractors, and permanent employees who might also be part of the team.

Being a temporary leader, and having the attitude of a permanent one, is a challenge accepted by an interim leader. In this case, an interim demonstrates relational savvy with internal employees reporting to the interim; this requires finding a balance of relationship building, professional leadership, and authority despite the "temporary" leader label. It is always advisable for an interim to approach this challenge by investing in team members as if the interim were the permanent leader, coach, and collaborator. In other words, the interim should not let the role's temporary status get in the way of attitude, commitment, and results.

Consider these examples:

Savvy Example: Coaching a team member as a respected equal

1. *Helen was in a supportive role that did not bring out the best in her; she was competent, but not confident. During the period of the interim leader's contract, Helen was encouraged into a role that played to her niche strengths and knowledge. She was invited to join the senior leadership team, even though she wasn't at the same grade as others – because she had a unique contribution. Over time, and often through many crises of confidence, Helen grew in credibility, poise, and influence. By the time the interim leader's contract finished, Helen was a respected equal in the senior leadership team as well as someone whose reputation was growing externally and internally.*

Savvy Example: Candid feedback and investing in a team member's development

2. *Saul had an overinflated view of his capability. He thought he should be at the top but did not have the expertise or leadership excellence to merit this recognition. To give the team a level playing field, Saul was asked to lead a couple of workstreams on a project, the same as other members of the team. Despite much coaching and support, Saul's ability to perform was insufficient. As time went on, Saul's development and capability were the focus of much investment on the part of the interim leader. At the same time, the interim managed Saul's expectations with a realistic view as to where he was on the growth continuum. On one occasion, Saul intentionally*

tried to embarrass the interim leader by presenting work he had plagiarized to show he was worthy of higher status. The client was in a culture where honor, seniority, and accolades mattered more than actual performance, application, and qualification. This culture compounded Saul's behavior and increased the interim's challenge. The interim leader had a frank conversation with Saul about his behavior. On completion of the interim's contract, Saul provided feedback to the client that in essence the interim leader had helped him to become a better human being – a worthwhile outcome!

These two examples illustrate the insight and judgments that an interim needs to make about staff and other stakeholders to develop a track record of effectiveness and deliver results. Leaving a client with a reputation as a savvy, effective leader is as important as a reputation for delivering successful outcomes. This concept is explored more in Chapter 9 (Legacy).

. . . .

It is important for the client and the interim leader to agree clear boundaries, expectations, and rules of engagement.

. . . .

Relational savvy is not only an opportunity for an interim leader to demonstrate expertise, sensitivity, and wisdom, it is also a challenge. An interim is by nature an achiever, fast-mover, and dynamic leader. Expecting an interim to passively work on a project in the corner is unrealistic. Most interims push for an audience with the C-Suite as a matter of course to inform their assignment's outcomes. Leveraging C-Suite exposure and project leadership is a test of maturity and judgment. It requires a high degree of stakeholder insight, professional timing, and critical reasoning. It is important for the client and the interim leader to agree clear boundaries, expectations, and rules of engagement. This ensures that the interim delivers results while tapping relationships that are critical and significant; the client can have total confidence in the interim's way of working while maintaining the over-sight of leadership.

Emotional intelligence is the heartbeat of relational savvy. Knowing oneself profoundly, understanding others in a deep way, and having an intuitive antenna to read context, are all part of being emotionally intelligent. Often the best interim leader is one who draws from his or her maturity, insight, and foresight to ensure that relationships support the mission and goals at hand, rather than undermine or damage them.

Relational savvy also requires an interim to assert him or herself in situations that require change. An interim's ability to bring objectivity and expertise are critical reasons why a client might hire an interim. The client may hire an interim to dislodge the status quo, or a paradigm of predictable internal leadership. In this case, an interim needs to grasp the challenge courageously and be savvy about relationship management. There's nothing smart or savvy about making a senior leader or peer look incompetent! There is everything smart about making them look valued. An interim often has a privileged position of being able to see and say things that others cannot. An interim's fresh perspective, based on years of experience, can often bring light in dark places.

. . . .

A fresh perspective, based on years of experience, can often bring light in dark places.

. . . .

An interim's ability to share candid reflections is a critical element of relational savvy. Since an interim does not seek a long-term career in a client organization, he or she can detect and share observations that others cannot. Given an interim's experience and the nature of the engagement, providing feedback to permanent leadership is an essential part of the interim's contribution. This includes cutting through the moaning of the team and a leader's ineffective behavior; it means that positive changes can be made. With savvy and skill, an interim handles relationships in a professional and respectful manner; this ensures that clients receive feedback positively. Whatever the scenario, an interim has the opportunity to make a difference to organizations by demonstrating relational savvy.

Cultural Savvy

How does an interim leader "read" the culture of an organization? "How things get done around here" is a useful definition of culture. All leaders, interims or otherwise, need to understand organizational culture to be effective.

An interim has to pick up on cultural savvy quickly to be successful. There is no time for an orientation program or to walk the corridors for weeks decoding cultural cues. Ignoring the culture, assuming one already knows best, is also inappropriate. An effective interim learns, for example, how things are communicated —when to pick up the phone rather than send an email, when to speak for five minutes rather than 30, and when cartoons on a PowerPoint slide are inappropriate. In addition to communication, an interim learns relational dynamics as part of the culture; this might include, for example, when an "open-door" policy requires one to syndicate information before walking through the open door. Clearly, there are many facets of culture for an interim to absorb, without having extended time for a full cultural immersion.

Schein describes culture in *Organizational Culture and Leadership* as operating at three levels: artefacts, espoused values, and the deepest level of basic assumptions. Observational skills are essential for understanding culture. It is important to understand the impact of artefacts, values, and assumptions in the way an organization operates, relationships are built, and work gets done.

- *Artefacts* represent the tangible, easily observable facets of organizational life. These include, for example, the physical fabric and layout of a building or office, and the organizational structure and policies.
- *Values* operate at a conscious level and dictate what the organization believes to be "good" or "bad".
- *Assumptions* are implicit, and they guide behavior, thinking, feeling, and perception.

Is the organization's espoused culture aligned with the purpose, mission, and goals? Some organizations have open, progressive, and positive cultures. What a great environment in which to get things done! Others are filled with political nuances, closed-door offices, and power games. Still other organizations have cultures that are elusive, even sinister, and demand superhuman sensitivity and skill from an interim leader who needs to accomplish certain goals.

Schein's description of culture reveals the subtleties that an interim may face and why an interim needs to learn to develop cultural savvy. He describes culture as: "a multidimensional, multifaceted phenomenon, not easily reduced to a few major dimensions."

Whatever the culture of an organization, it is critical for an interim to understand it as soon as possible. This will shape how the interim achieves key objectives. Ignoring "how things get done" in an organization will cloud an interim's ability to build effective relationships and have an impact. In fact, an interim leader likely has more cultural savvy than most leaders since he or she has been exposed to so many organizational cultures. An interim moves between organizations across industry sectors, sizes, and geographies. In his or her varied experience, an interim works with highly effective leaders and teams, as well as some that are not competent. It is likely that an interim leader has been party to many cultural change initiatives. An interim learns to "read the signs" to interpret the culture. An interim also needs to be quick on the uptake to fulfil the expectations of an interim assignment—fast, excellent results. Through experience, an interim develops an affinity for understanding culture and a keen sense of cultural savvy.

. . . .

An interim leader has more cultural savvy than most leaders since he or she has been exposed to so many organizational cultures.

. . . .

Here are contrasting examples of cultural savvy:

Savvy Example: Managing across cultural conflicts

1. *An interim leader was contracted to lead an internal team in a company based in the Middle East. There were two unique cultures in play – one centered around the ex-patriots and the other around the indigenous population. The ex-patriots were largely there for the money, weren't*

particularly motivated to deliver change, and protected their positions as much as possible. The indigenous population was steeped in positional power based on tribal affiliations. They also weren't particularly motivated (or necessarily able) to deliver change, but they were eager to take on more senior leadership roles. Over a period of just over a year the interim proposed major changes to the functional team. There were, however, real difficulties in implementing these changes as the prevailing culture did not accommodate the impact they would bring. The contract eventually reached a stalemate. For the interim this was clearly an opportunity to design change but hampered by a fundamental challenge: implementation in an unforgiving culture.

Savvy Example: Unified cultural support

2. *An interim contract was focused on the delivery of a three-year development program for a company's future partner pipeline. This company had invested heavily in creating an open, creative culture that pervaded from the CEO all the way to the interns. This resulted in a receptive environment in which to propose designs with creativity, challenge, and change. All employees appeared to be unified, facing the same direction and wanting to be successful, with the culture playing a major role. Openness, thankfulness, and humor were a daily experience. The interim successfully completed the assignment over a number of years in an environment rich with satisfaction, learning, and challenge.*

Interim leaders often display chameleon-like attributes in

learning and leveraging corporate culture, as well as being authentic and true to themselves. Adapting within cultures to be impactful is a critical aspect of successful interim leadership.

Case Study: Restructure Business and Build for Future Growth

How does a savvy interim leader build trust, understanding, and permission to influence the strategic growth of a client organization?

1. Client Context
UK arm of the world's largest building materials distribution company with group turnover in excess of £14billion. Division Build Center (UK) – 500 depots with annual turnover of £550m.

2. Assignment
Interim Managing Director reporting to the UK CEO.
- The build center brand had grown by acquisition over several years which masked a decline in the annual like-for-like revenues and an increase in costs, resulting in a significant decline in profitability. The interim MD was hired to reverse this trend. There was no clear sense as to what was driving the underperformance nor how to reverse it.
- The interim MD was hired primarily because of previous experience in the sector/industry for several years and management of a multi-site business on a larger scale.

3. Results
- Interim MD facilitated the discussion with the executive team to the point where they realized that the business

had lost its identity and vision as a result of the numerous acquisitions; there was no clear customer proposition, and the team didn't feel empowered to change it.

- Once this was clear, the rest was relatively easy. With a new vision for the business and a clear customer proposition and structure for fulfilment, the team could drive the necessary changes for themselves.
- The assignment lasted one year which is slightly longer than anticipated; this was a result of the scale of the business. At the end of Year 1 revenues were increasing in high-single digits and costs were under control, managed by the depots themselves rather than from the top.
- As a result of the success, the Interim MD was asked to carry out a similar process for another division of the business which also took one year.

4. **Benefits of an Interim Leader Solution**
   - Businesses always experience difficulties. Interim Managing Directors and CEO's are never brought in to maintain the status quo. Therefore, a background in managing change and understanding the relationship dynamics in a change situation are prerequisites to executing the role.
   - Businesses sometimes lose sight of their customers. As the business underperforms there is a tendency to look inwards for someone to blame. Looking inside is never the solution — a bit like re-arranging the deckchairs on the *Titanic*.
   - Incumbents can become invested in underperformance and look for reasons to explain the situation. In other words, they identify with the numbers rather than take responsibility for them. In the case in question, this had

reached an institutionalized level where each branch manager had to complete a form on a monthly basis explaining why the numbers were "off". This could range from competition, weather, lack of stock, price, etc. The business was putting more effort into explaining the performance than correcting it. This is one of the main reasons an interim leader is so successful. He or she is not invested in the numbers and can look at the situation much more objectively. By accepting the performance and not seeking to rationalize it, an interim can get the team to focus on the future. At the same time, you cannot make the past wrong. By doing so you are in fact blaming some of the people in the room. Creating the right context by doing both of these things the interim got the team to think about creating a different future.

- By definition, an interim is new to the business and might even be new to the industry. This means that he or she does not come with preconceptions about what the problems are and how to fix them. This leads to an open and engaging discussion with the managers who run the business and the role becomes about facilitating the team to find solutions rather than giving them "prefab" solutions. An effective, savvy interim can develop the solution from within the business rather than having it imposed from outside.

- Finally, an interim can overstay his or her welcome, i.e., begin to take on some of the characteristics of the host client. Hire an interim, but don't let them stay too long.

CHAPTER 6

Critical

Critical – a turning point or especially important juncture where definite change is occurring.

Many interim leaders consider themselves among the best business change leaders. For this reason, they can be incredibly influential in organizational development. As Jim Collins says in *Good to Great,* "Put your best people on your biggest opportunities, not your biggest problems." Not only should client organizations consider interims as "best people" to tackle critical projects, but interims are also likely to target critical opportunities that provide the type of challenge they seek. In *The Interim Manager* Clutterbuck and Dearlove note, "These are usually confident social animals with exacting criteria for selecting a case for treatment."

This chapter defines the kinds of scenarios in which an interim leader is most effective – critical interventions essential to the health and growth of the organization. It explores the reasons why the engagement of an interim leader within the context of critical organizational needs is often the best solution, one where experience, results, and pace are essential.

An interim is not a "business-as-usual" leader. In fact, an interim often chooses to move on from an organization once the environment is dominated by the status quo. As discussed in previous chapters, an interim is the architect of his or her own career and is not interested in employment continuity for the sake of accruing benefits, climbing a corporate ladder, or coasting through a period of organizational consolidation. As Besondy and Travis state in *Leadership on Demand*, "They provide the ability to execute new initiatives professionally, generating results while leaving infrastructure for someone else to come in and manage when they're gone."

The reasons why an organization engages an interim leader are often critical to the evolutionary stage in which the organization finds itself. This might include, for example, the need for integration and transformation following an acquisition, or when a major strategic objective is dependent on successful, time-sensitive implementation. Clients often regard an interim as a trusted advisor to assist them through a critical phase in their organizational development. As David Maister states in *The Trusted Advisor*, "The trusted advisor is the person the client turns to when an issue first arises, often in times of great urgency: a crisis, a triumph, or a defeat."

. . . .

Clients often regard an interim as a trusted advisor to assist them through a critical phase in their organizational development.

. . . .

It might seem strange to suggest that an interim is seen as a trusted advisor, especially since an interim is not a permanent resource or consultant-on-a-shelf. This privilege of earning a client's trust often stems from a previous relationship, recommendation, or the accelerated impact an interim makes in a new client organization. Whatever the source of the trust, clients view an interim as a critical asset to help leadership steer through organizational challenges.

An interim is a critical resource for critical times in organizational development. Consider the following examples.

Critical Example: New client transition

1. *The interim leader had been working with a client for nine months. Realizing that the contract would soon be coming to an end, the interim had also been speaking to another client who was lining up a major organizational-change program that had a critical timeframe in which delivery was essential. This new client asked the interim if he would come and work for them to help them deliver a global outsourcing project with multiple, interdependent workstreams that had launched the previous month. Having sensed that the existing client's work was moving to an integration phase, the interim informed the client that he would not be renewing the contract once the term was completed, a timeframe of a few days. This was an awkward moment as the client had hoped to extend*

the interim's contract. Once the client had processed this news, the client and the interim parted company with a mutual understanding and an appreciation that this change benefited both parties. The interim joined the new client the following week. The success of this transition hinged on the interim's ability to engage in carefully managed, professional, and candid conversations — critical at times like this. The interim avoided the kind of contentious and awkward conversation that leaves a disappointed client behind. In most contract negotiations a "no surprises" approach is taken, indicating intentions as far in advance as possible. In this instance, the interim leader acted with integrity and professionalism, and was free, both contractually and in good conscience, to commence the new client's critical project. Engaging with the new client at that specific time was a crucial part of meeting critical-path timelines, and the interim delivered his part of the project successfully. This interim had the right skill set and was immediately available, which often intersects with a critical client requirement.

Critical Example: Aligning with changing organizational realities

2. *An interim leader was asked to lead an engineering academy and take it from a highly successful legacy focus to a future-focused and professionally empowered organization. Sometimes an interim has the critical skills required to undertake a project even if he or she hasn't worked in the specific industry before. In this instance, the interim had a strong track-record of business, strategy, and team leadership skills to embark on the project. The client also needed someone to align the academy within a*

dynamically changing external environment. Being able to grasp the governmental, technical, organizational, and legal implications of the challenge and imagine a new academy were all critical elements of the assignment. The client could not wait for the academy to evolve. It had to align with changing legislation, technology, and commercial realities. Clearly the need for the interim's leadership and transformation were critical if the academy was to provide the organization with a competitive and enhanced capability to succeed.

• •

Clients hire an interim to shift the paradigm. An interim's self-assurance to deliver this is based on experience, courage, and maturity.

• •

Clients hire an interim to shift the paradigm. An interim's self-assurance to deliver this is based on experience, courage, and maturity. An interim leader is eager to take on responsibility for significant challenges. The higher the mountain or the deeper the valley, the more an interim is confident in his or her commitment to make a difference. An interim is not afraid of client demands like, "The system needs a root and branch overhaul", "Timescales are ridiculously short", or "This will take a miracle to fix". Indeed, an interim's motivation is often fueled by the critical challenges that others might think twice about. Clients may seek an interim to tackle specific challenges that move an organization towards a broader outcome. These challenges are often fast-paced, multiple projects within an overall strategy. This is consistent with Robert Schaffer's observations in *High-Impact Consulting*, "In high-impact consulting, rather than an overall solution at once, the aim is to carve off a series of rapid-cycle attacks."

· ·
**"The results of the interim leader are measurable –
they show up in the financials." Richard Lindenmuth,
*The Outside the Box Executive***
· ·

An interim engagement does not simply provide temporary coverage for organizational continuity; it is often an opportunity for applied expertise to drive an organization forward in a critical capability or at a critical juncture of organizational development. Whatever the context, an interim's contribution invariably delivers against metrics that reflect the health of the organization. As Richard Lindenmuth notes in *The Outside the Box Executive*, "The results of the interim leader are measurable – they show up in the financials."

In what critical contexts are interims especially successful?

- Crisis or turnaround management
- Organizational growth
- Integration following a merger or acquisition
- Reducing cost and increasing value
- Raising the bar on performance and expectations

Crisis or Turnaround Management

Sometimes organizations find themselves in situations in which incumbent leaders have either proved incompetent or hit a brick wall. Organizations may have run aground in a sea of intense competition, may have failed to keep up with technology, products, or markets, or may need a cash injection to get moving again. In these instances, an interim can make a critical contribution by turning around a bad situation quickly. This can be particularly relevant in private equity or venture-capital-backed organizations; the investors seek a quick turnaround in the company performance. This requires the experience, agility, and insight of an interim leader.

Critical Example: Immediate leadership program turnaround

1. *A client needed help with a high-potential leadership program that was on the rocks. The previous leader of this program had left the program in a state where a lot of the budget had been spent, but little value had accrued. Turning the situation around quickly was critical to rescuing the credibility of the program, maintaining the organizational commitment to the participants, and ensuring a leadership pipeline fit for the firm's future direction. Re-assessing the objectives of the program, re-aligning the design, engaging internal leaders to deliver keynotes, and conducting candid conversations with the participants as well as their managers, were all actions that required immediate attention. The interim ensured that the program recovered into a high-value initiative that delivered excellent results.*

Critical Example: Successful program delivery

2. *A client had initiated a leadership development program across the organization. The program had reached a point in its lifecycle where there was a significant risk that the launch was not going to be successful. To add to this predicament, the lead designer had left the company. The interim bolstered a potentially failing program, wrapped it in strict project management disciplines, and created a credible design with a delivery partner organization; the program was launched successfully and went*

on to deliver outstanding results.

Critical Example: Managing multiple stakeholders

3. *The challenge of designing a future-focused development strategy for a group of professional experts in the
medical field had resulted in the design lead providing a disjointed and academically focused proposal.
Unpacking the work accomplished to-date, proposing
an alternative, innovative strategy to deliver pragmatic
outcomes, and maintaining the commitment of multiple
stakeholder groups, were all part of the critical challenges the interim faced to rescue this initiative. The interim
relied on speed of assessment, savvy management of
transitional sensitivities, and an innovative approach that
inspired the client groups impacted.*

All three of these examples illustrate potential crisis points that
an interim can address through swift action.

. . . .

**An interim's ability to troubleshoot, leverage
experience, and design outstanding solutions
in short timeframes under pressure
distinguishes an interim from other leaders.**

. . . .

Why is the option of engaging an experienced interim leader
to address a crisis most likely to deliver a successful outcome?

• An interim's ability to troubleshoot, leverage experience,
and design outstanding solutions in short timeframes under pressure distinguishes an interim from other leaders.

What options are least likely to deliver a successful outcome in a crisis?

- Trying to bolster the situation with an internal resource – if one is available
- Bringing in a consultancy who will likely wrap the project with additional cost and management; there is no guarantee that an intelligent consultant will have the experience or savvy to address the critical situation.
- Outsourcing the challenge to a vendor; the speed of organizational understanding and program integration might easily become tangled with the commercial ambitions of the vendor.

One of the significant advantages of hiring an interim to handle a crisis is that he or she is an experienced leader who has been through similar situations. An interim has battle scars from crisis management and like a first-responder in a disaster zone, is objective, decisive, and has emotional stability shaped from years of being in the front line. An interim brings a steady hand to level the potential chaos of a crisis.

Organizational Growth

An interim appreciates the investment made in hiring him (or her) to deliver significant impact. This often happens when organizations are on the cusp of strategic change or embarking on growth initiatives. Clearly, these are critical moments in organizational development.

The following examples illustrate this:

Critical Example: Leading a broad range of initiatives

1. *A client had laid out a very ambitious strategy of doubling revenue within the next five years. The CEO did not, however, believe that the organization had the leadership to deliver this; this included the issues of alignment, capability, and application. The client asked the interim leader to lead a series of initiatives, including a leadership conference, board assessment, organizational design, leadership development, and performance process improvement. Clearly, the range of these initiatives was a challenge to resource. This experienced interim, like most interims, was used to leading a broad range of initiatives, had deep experience in the discipline, and the stretch capability to apply himself across a wide range of needs. Delivering the needs of the client in this instance was clearly an opportunity for the interim to partner in the investment being made to grow the organization. An interim is unafraid of the return on investment that his or her contribution requires. Indeed, an interim is often inspired to prove that his or her contribution is essential to successfully meeting targets and goals.*

Critical Example: Unified vision for all employees

2. *The client asked the interim leader to align every employee behind a single strategy and vision with complementary personal development goals within six weeks. The CEO, who had ambitious plans to grow the company, spelled out this requirement. Defining an approach to achieve this was obviously a challenge for the interim, especially in an asset management firm where staff*

could not easily leave their desks to undertake develop-
ment. The interim met this challenge by providing a flex-
ible program of half-day and full-day interventions, led
by senior leaders and with clear deliverables that would
ensure the goals were reached within the timescales.
Clearly, the opportunity to contribute to a critical ele-
ment of the organizational growth strategy was both a
challenge and incredibly rewarding for this interim.

Engaging an interim to inject pace, innovation, and direction to a growth initiative, is often rewarded by results that meet or exceed the goal. Indeed, this is the nature of the contract. Even if an interim is responsible for only part of the bigger picture, an interim's contribution ensures that overall objectives are met —and exceeded. Organizational growth depends on critical resources pulling together. Having an interim deliver against high aspirations is an effective way to build momentum and reassure senior leadership who have the vision and ambition for success. For an interim, delivering against these immediate objectives often means a contract extension to support the client's additional objectives.

• •

**Engaging an interim to inject pace, innovation,
and direction to a growth initiative is often
rewarded by results that meet or exceed the goal.**

• •

Integration Following a Merger or Acquisition

Anyone who has been through a merger or acquisition knows the pressures: emotions are stretched, workloads increased, and impacts are magnified. An interim leader brings immense value to the process of organizational mergers or acquisitions. An interim offers a wealth of experience and a savvy ability to navigate sensitive relationships and critical projects.

Mergers and acquisitions are an intense environment in which an interim adds value due to the interim's keen insights, professionalism, and fearless wisdom. The mandate is often simple: risks need to be minimized and opportunities maximized. This is a perfect fit for an interim. In fact, navigating the fast moving "white-water" environments of mergers and acquisitions attracts an interim leader. This is reciprocated by organizational leaders who recognize that interims are a highly credible and effective resource to leverage at times like this. Experience and sound judgment, paired with pace and incisiveness, are far more critical during a merger or acquisition than considerations of job protection or preservation of culture. As Richard Lindenmuth says in *The Outside the Box Executive*, "Mergers & Acquisitions is an area where interim leaders thrive. It calls on all of their skills, beginning with active listening to the thoughts, ideas, and concerns of both the acquiring company and the company being acquired." An interim is successful and objective in the roles of facilitator, arbiter, strategist, and intermediary.

. . . .

An interim is very successful and objective in the roles of facilitator, arbiter, strategist, and intermediary.

. . . .

Why is an interim leader valued during a merger or acquisition?

- Objective perspective
- Savvy relationship skills

- Experienced crisis manager
- Decisive leader
- Agile and strategic amidst pressures and short timeframes

Reducing Cost and Increasing Value

Organizations seek the Holy Grail of reducing costs while increasing value. This requirement is a classic opportunity for an interim to showcase his or her skills on behalf of the organization.

Consider the following example:

Critical Example: Transform online educational tools

> *An interim leader was asked by a telecommunications client to transform their online learning environment. This was critical to the client, given the need for many of the client's employees to achieve certification on diverse technical products as well as the need to provide distributed learning tools across a virtual workforce. There was an incumbent provider for these learning needs, but the impact of the learning was low. The research and analysis provided by the interim resulted in a significant outcome: engaging a new vendor with much more content, an enhanced, customized hosted environment, a full-time project management resource, all within a reduced budget. Clearly the interim maximized on this opportunity to add value and impact to the client organization, while reducing costs.*

An interim leader has typically been around the block a few times. He or she has the professional insight to know what "good value" looks like – hopefully accentuated by looking in the mirror at their own skill set. An interim's contributions and impact to an organization adds value on many levels and exceeds client expectations.

How does an interim add value?

- Professional credibility
- Listens and understands what the client needs
- Exceeds the client's expectations
- Delivers significant results in short timeframes
- Free of constraints of organizational politics
- Objective ability to envision change, paradigm shift
- Experienced with cost reduction and vendor negotiations
- Motivated to succeed
- Confidence inspires senior leadership and teams
- Single leadership resource who manages organizational systems and teams

When it comes to adding value to an organization while identifying opportunities to streamline and cut costs, an interim puts the client's best interest first. An interim brings not only the benefits of expertise, but also the professional credibility of an experienced leader who knows how to assess solutions and vendors, as well as understand the impact of his or her actions across an organization.

An interim is an experienced leader who knows how to assess solutions and vendors, as well as understand the impact of his or her actions across an organization.

Raising the Bar on Performance and Expectations

What does it mean to raise the bar? To reach stretch goals? To set higher standards of accountability? There are times when an organization knows a leap forward is needed and that it is a critical mistake not to take this leap. Raising the bar for such an organization is critical to changing its culture and disturbing paradigms that might otherwise cause stagnation. Often, the incumbent leadership of an organization sees this but may need support to execute the needed changes. An interim offers an objective perspective that can further trigger the perception that a change is needed. To raise the bar, interims bring a wealth of experience, and the ability to intervene in a way that is tailored to the organization, with unique expression. An interim leader also understands the urgency and need for action, especially when the organization is at a critical juncture.

There are strategies for raising the bar that add value and deliver impact. In the sport of high jumping, for example, courageous jumpers shrewdly forgo incremental raises in the bar's height, to save themselves for the larger leaps —jumps with higher measurements and therefore points and a higher score. There is, of course, risk associated with this strategy; if the athlete fails to clear the bar at a greater height, then he or she will suffer penalties or fall behind competitors who cleared lower jumps. The same is true for an interim leader, who must commit to strategic, calculated risks in delivering as high a "jump" – stretch goals — as possible to achieve a winning position and significant impact and results. An interim collaborates effectively with a client to plan such strategy and provides solid and talented capability to deliver stretch goals as well as those that are clearly achievable.

Consider the following examples:

Critical Example: Raising the bar on negotiation strategies

1. *An interim leader was asked to coach a Chief Human Resource Officer in negotiations with trade unions over changes to a performance-management system. The climate of these negotiations had always been adversarial, and the motivation for change had therefore always been incremental at best. Taking the bit between the teeth, the interim recommended a change to the system that was quite a leap – raising the bar. This involved convincing the CHRO that the arguments surrounding this change could be powerfully articulated to demonstrate greater fairness, objective rigor, and personal benefits. The arguments won the day!*

Critical Example: A convincing ROI for succession planning

2. *Working with a client CEO, the interim was faced with the challenge of convincing the CEO of the value of investing in an assessment/development program for his senior leaders. Until this point, a conservative approach had been taken in this respect, but the interim brought a compelling proposition to deliver effective succession planning and development. The challenge was even greater given that the CEO was an accountant. The interim's strategy included engaging an external organization that specialized in research and case studies to demonstrate Return On Investment (ROI), a smart initiative. At the end of a day spent evaluating the potential investment, the CEO signed off on the program – the interim clearly articulated the value and the ROI was convincing.*

It often takes the experience and technique of a seasoned interim to influence the mindset of other leaders to stretch beyond the ordinary. An interim often needs to break through the fear that holds back progress. Being bold enough to inject critical momentum for clients is a significant role for an interim leader.

Case Study: Roll-out of CRM (Customer Relationship Management) System

How do interim leaders deliver projects critical to the organization's success and engage the existing workforce behind these initiatives?

1. **Client Context**

<u>The client is a B2C and B2B financial services provider</u>. Annual revenue $4.3bn. Number of employees 17,000. An impending roll-out of a new CRM system required a review of the sales and marketing organization, which also required that the interim bring significant project management capability.

2. **Assignment**

The original trigger for this assignment was the looming global roll-out of Salesforce.com ('SFDC'), combined with the desire to address the sales and marketing shortcomings identified by an extensive review of the region's business development capability. Reporting to the Regional Managing Director, the <u>12-month interim assignment as a Program Director for the SFDC Program</u> had a number of key deliverables:

- Ahead of the SFDC rollout, work with the Sales Effectiveness team to prepare countries for the SFDC rollout by creating a common language, consistent job roles, and a client-centric way of selling

- Analyse key business-development review recommendations to determine which needs to be: addressed in the Sales Effectiveness programme; addressed subsequently; and which could be incorporated in one of the above. Recommend routes to deliver the chosen recommendations
- Oversee the successful rollout of SFDC, migrating countries from previous versions of SFDC and those on other CRM platforms with equal success
- Transfer appropriate skills and experience to team members with whom the interim was sharing the journey

3. **Results**
   - As far as the client was concerned, not having any leaders and Country Heads complaining to him about SFDC was enough of a success for him to personally justify the investment in an effective senior interim.
   - Aside from the specific delivery of the objectives above, other success measures included the effective rollout of the transformation of the sales and marketing operations of a pilot country.
   - Stakeholder management was a key success measure. The Program Director needed to ensure that the Program met the needs of three levels of senior managers:
     - o Global business unit leaders
     - o Country heads
     - o Regional functional heads (Finance, Sales, etc.)
   - Finding consensus across countries on Sales KPIs, and agreeing and documenting the resulting balanced scorecard, were seen as key success measures.

All these objectives were achieved during the life of the assignment.

4. Benefits of an Interim Solution

Like many other sales and marketing assignments, there are elements of experience, knowledge, and insight that a senior interim practitioner brings:

- Pace – An interim's focus on delivering a specific set of objectives within a specific timeframe drives a pace of delivery an internal resource cannot match.
- Leadership – An interim typically has operated in multiple environments with differing teams and is expert at motivating those he or she works with to getting "the best" from them.
- Knowledge – An interim has an in-depth practitioner's knowledge of the function (in this case, sales and marketing) as well as a proven network of service providers that are able to deliver specific services (e.g. sales training) in support of an overall program.
- Flexibility – An interim is usually organizationally agile, able to judge the right approach to take with stakeholders and staff to achieve specific objectives in a shorter period of time than the organization believes is possible.
- Network – An interim has to build networks quickly within often complex organizations. He or she has to understand the nuances between the functions and matrices so essential to the work that gets done in larger organizations or, conversely, be able to do it all (single-handedly) in smaller organizations.

CHAPTER 7

Impact

Impact - to have a direct and strong effect on someone or something

A recent YouTube video features millennials propelling through their education to make an impact in the world, only to find that the workplace is more mundane than they had envisioned. It is a deeply human impulse to want to make changes for the common good and receive praise for doing so. It is also human to underestimate the drive and expertise needed to bring about such change. There are of course those at the other end of the spectrum, who shudder at the thought of making an impact. These individuals want to remain under the radar as they do their jobs, take home a paycheck, and live a quiet life. For an interim leader, having an impact is more than an attitude that one brings to work. It is a career choice.

An interim leader is committed to making an impact, and has the expertise and resolve needed to meet challenges along the way. As this chapter explores, making an impact differentiates an interim leader from other leadership options. It sets a standard for the best interim leaders. As Giles Hutchins notes in *Future Fit*, "The best people want to feel a meaningful connection with the value they create, rather than feeling like lost cogs enslaved in the monolith of machine mentality."

An interim is seldom hired to augment staff numbers, or cover for temporarily absent leaders, such as those on medical or family leave; an interim is sometimes hired to bridge a resourcing gap between permanent hires. An interim makes the most impact, however, when intentionally hired to deliver specific results that require a leader with experience and dynamism. As Richard Lindenmuth states in *The Outside the Box Executive*, "An interim leader will bring focus to an organization."

. . . .
An interim makes the most impact when intentionally hired to deliver results that require a leader with experience and dynamism.
. . . .

An interim leader is frequently hired as a "big-splash" leader. The reason he or she chooses an interim career is because other careers have not been fulfilling; an interim's greatest value to organizations is to lead fast, meaningful, and distinctive change. These high-impact changes need to carry significant organizational meaning and value to warrant tapping an interim's expertise. As the Confederation of British Industry suggest in their business guide, *Interim Executive Management*, "The job of an interim is to leave the business in better shape than he or she found it, and it's not just about the short term."

It is essential when considering "impact" to embrace the "high-impact paradigm" described by Robert Schaffer in *High-Impact Consulting*, ". . .this is based on the premise that although the consultant's expert solutions are vital to the success of a consulting project, it is just as vital for consultants to help clients absorb, use, and benefit from these solutions." As well as delivering solutions, an interim ensures that the client is suitably equipped to implement and integrate them, even if the interim is not directly involved in the ongoing evolution of the organization.

Consider the following questions that clients asked a savvy interim (the author) at the start of four separate interim assignments. Each carries an urgent challenge, demanding impact from the interim that is on par with a disaster response.

"Our whole leadership development framework is broken and doesn't work. Can you help fix it?"

"Our high potential leadership program is on the rocks. Can you rescue it and make it fit for purpose?"

"Our engineering academy delivers legacy requirements but is not future-focused. Can you change it?"

"Our global development framework has to be transformed within six months. Can you help do it?"

Anyone who shrinks from the pressure of walking into

high-impact zones or finds high-bar challenges daunting, should not consider an interim leader career. An interim leader demonstrates utmost professionalism under such pressures, partnering with clients to make a positive impact. As David Maister describes it in *The Trusted Advisor*, "The essence of professionalism lies not in distinguishing ourselves from our clients, but in aligning with them to improve their situations – inclusive professionalism."

· ·

An interim is an expert at shifting paradigms, energizing changes in direction, and adding tangible, significant value.

· ·

Making an impact is about shifting paradigms, energizing changes in direction, fixing things, and adding tangible, significant value. This is increasingly relevant in an environment that requires organizations to be at their most agile. McGovern and Russell discuss this in *A New Brand of Expertise*, "It is almost impossible to predict what is around the next corner. It is therefore essential to create organizations that are agile enough to alter their skills mix, capacity, and focus at a moment's notice." There aren't many organizations who wouldn't want this ability to add impetus, at least from time to time, in specific directions, if not across the board. An interim is agile, highly qualified to make an immediate impact. As the Confederation of British Industry say in their business guide, *Interim Executive Management*, "Stepping into an organization on day one, high-caliber interims will establish immediate credibility."

How do interims make an impact?

- Dynamic
- Insightful
- Results-focused
- Courageous

Dynamic Impact

An interim is often driven to stimulate, provoke, transform, and deliver. This doesn't mean that he or she is a walking time bomb or a perpetual chaos creator. An interim is restless when a status quo descends on an organization and seeks opportunities to make a difference. This can be opportune for organizations.

. . . .

An interim is restless when a status quo descends on an organization and seeks opportunities to make a difference.

. . . .

Sir Leonard Peach, ex-chairman of IBM, reflects in Russell and Daniell's *Interim Management,* "A brief injection of new thinking and energy may provide the incentive, relief or quality of thinking which provide energy, stimulus or accelerated results which all organizations require from time to time."

Being dynamic doesn't mean being a loose cannon. An interim is a highly nuanced, tuned leader. The best interim leaders have been shaped by the fires of organizational experience and senior leadership responsibility. An interim leader has made a career choice: to offer expertise to organizations to make a difference—an impact —in a short timeframe. An organization or senior leader hiring an interim needs to appreciate the dynamic nature of the beast. As is the case in many professions, not all interims are the same. An effective, competent interim leader is committed to the client to deliver on clear objectives and make a significant contribution in doing so.

An interim leader contrasts vividly to a permanent hire or consultant in the first few days of tenure. For example, it is not unusual for a new recruit in organizations to undergo a slow ramp-up to effectiveness, including at a leadership level. This may begin with a two-week long orientation program and a period of networking, learning, and reading. Consultants often conduct numerous brain-storming and planning sessions, sometimes presenting the client with a recommendation as to how their methodology delivers against requirements – subject to further debate with the client. An interim typically produces the first strategic assessment with initial recommendations at the end of the first week, if not the second. This is how dynamic and proactive an interim leader can be.

Impact Example: Fast and dynamic contribution; change leadership

> The interim leader commenced a project with a client with the requirement to lead multiple workstreams, sub-teams of employees, a complex outsourcing relationship, and the onboarding of new team members. The interim had to deliver critical projects in short timeframes. These types of multiple demands across a wide range of skills energizes an interim. In this case, the interim conducted his initial assessment and arranged to meet the client at the end of the second week in the organization. The purpose of the meeting was to present a proposed strategy paper to address all the

issues outlined above. The client was surprised at the interim's speed of understanding, scope of analysis, comprehensive delivery plan, and savvy instinct. This is a dynamic interim in action.

A successful interim demonstrates dynamic intent, a sharp intellect, and an infectious enthusiasm to make an impact. An interim's appetite for challenge is as great as his or her capacity to deliver it.

Insightful Impact

What is insight? Perception? The ability to see with X-ray vision? It is one of the most critical of interim attributes. An interim is sometimes required to expose issues that might otherwise not be addressed by an organization. This takes insight. As Jim Collins states in *Good to Great*, "Leadership does not begin with just vision. It begins with getting people to confront the brutal facts and to act on the implications." Sometimes these "brutal facts" are brought to light by an interim who can see things with fresh perspective and deep insight into root causes. Of course, insight without a clue as to what to do after shining a light on an issue is of limited value. An interim pairs insight with action - the ability to interpret and execute a coherent, articulate response. This is immensely valuable in addressing organizational, cultural, financial, and relational challenges.

. . . .

"Brutal facts" are brought to light by an interim who is able to see things with fresh perspective and deep insight into root causes.

. . . .

An interim leader demonstrates his or her insight into all aspects of an organization, including relationships, culture, strategy, results, team dynamics, politics, and finances. It is like being able to scan the horizon and quickly assess weather patterns – both for tomorrow's forecast and the long-range outlook. Another analogy might be that of using a small aperture setting to focus on specifics, without losing the broader panorama. An interim's experience informs a decisive, mature assessment of an organization's environment, including threats and opportunities. As David Maister notes in *The Trusted Advisor,* this assessment can be accomplished through, "illustration, asking questions, listening, showing an interest, and showing appreciation." Through observant conversations with clients, the interim, as described in Chapter 5 (Savvy), gains the insight and understanding needed to make a lasting impact.

. . . .

An interim's experience informs a decisive, mature assessment of an organization's environment, including threats and opportunities.

. . . .

It is no surprise that cultivating and managing relationships is essential for developing insight. Relationships, in addition to the quality of the work itself, make or break a contract. This is true in any environment and especially so for an interim, who must quickly develop insight into relationships to avoid being played, exploited, or blind-sided. The following example illustrates this:

Impact Example: Navigating relationships

An interim leader was hired by the Chief Human

Resource Officer to focus on a specific project. The critical client for the work, however, was ultimately the Chief Executive Officer. The interim's relationship with the CEO was as important as the one with the CHRO, if not more so. Managing these two relationships with wisdom, openness, and accountability, was a significant part of the interim's role. The interim needed to understand who to connect with, when, and about what. The interim also had to navigate the relationships by knowing it was vital to keep both in the loop and being savvy when the CEO asked for a meeting without the CHRO (it was a critical time of transition). It was critical that the interim developed insight into how two critical stakeholders worked together. The situation needed the interim to interact with them to achieve successful results and impact.

There are some who consider insight to be the predominant domain of intuitive types. Yet, all are gifted with some insight and simply need to consciously flex this muscle to strengthen it. Insight builds on intuition as well as experience. Being able to recognize root causes or trends, detecting dependencies, and understanding implications are all areas of insight. Of course, the insight that an interim gains quickly is different than insight distilled over a long period of time and through many experiences. Both are useful for an interim to share with a client; the former can be shared through on-the-spot judgment, observation, and instinct, and the latter through an interim's analysis of more complex organizational dynamics.

Results-focused Impact

"Begin with the end in mind" is one of Charles Handy's mantras often quoted in leadership circles. It is certainly how most interims take on the challenge of a contract. As Robert Schaffer states in *High-Impact Consulting*, "In the high-impact consulting paradigm, clients and consultants take aim from the first moment at achieving some tangible results. Not programs. Not systems. Not reports. Not recommendations. Not studies with better answers. Not strategy formulations. None of these, unless they inherently include the delivery of some measurable bottom-line results."

"What would success look like?" "How would you measure completion of the task?" These questions are other ways of identifying the intent of an intervention. An interim is typically less concerned with long-term issues of organizational positioning and operational efficiency than with leading change to meet a client's immediate need. However, there are instances where an interim is asked to map a long-term strategic focus and fill in the gaps with short-term deliverables. It is often the big picture that frames the work of an interim. An interim leader's experience, insight, and focus on results means he or she delivers on tactical challenges while developing a broader strategic direction. An interim is motivated by results, not tenure. He or she has a professional balance that offers a delivery-oriented perspective rather than one offering only observation or recommendation.

An interim's reward is to deliver beyond the expectations of the client. Although, as Alasdair Drysdale points out in *The Interim Director*, "There are times when you consider that the work done is inadequate, but the client insists that you've done what he asks." There are some clients who simply aren't as advanced as the interim, and try as he or she may, the client wants a vanilla solution even when the interim recommends something more sophisticated. In these cases, an interim needs to focus on delivering targeted results without getting distracted by other organizational issues. As Peter Drucker notes in *The Effective Executive*, "Effective executives do not splinter themselves. They concentrate on one task if at all possible."

. . . .

An interim leader's fulfillment is not tethered to a prestigious role.

. . . .

An interim is not building a career with a client organization. Yet frequently, client organizations ask the interim to join them on a permanent basis (the organization would pay a fee to an agency if that is how the interim was introduced). Most committed interim leaders decline such an invitation to join the permanent workforce. Why? An interim leader's fulfillment is not tethered to a prestigious role in an organization's senior ranks, but in delivering great work with results that make an impact for the benefit of the organization and its employees. These two outcomes are not mutually exclusive, but an interim is more motivated to move on to another client and repeat a high-impact intervention than build a career with continuity of employment. Another motivation for an interim is repeated contact with clients over a period of years and the satisfaction of learning about the impact of the interim's work on client organizations and employees. There are many clients that have had successful experiences with interims and the impact, often innovative changes, are still in place. This is an accolade and an affirmation—the interim's judgment and execution were spot on!

Courageous Impact

An interim leader often lands in situations in which he or she needs to quickly assess the challenges, much like a decisive military leader; this requires not only courageous proposals, but courageous action. An interim is often confident and comfortable doing this, given his or her experience and propensity to action. An interim chose an interim career; this means the interim has the courage needed to make an impact. After all, not all leaders are comfortable with the uncertainty an interim learns to master, including the changing sources of paychecks, networking widely to win new business, maintaining professional relevance through self-development, and taking on new projects in new organizations, often in the face of severe challenges.

An interim is typically self-assured. This is not just an innate personality trait, but a result of a successful track record. An interim's courage and confidence are contagious, and clients experience it as well. To survive, an interim leader earns a reputation of delivering great quality work, building professional relationships, and showing flexibility and tenacity in their approach to work. Having the confidence to take on organizational and people issues is a given for an interim. As Alasdair Drysdale points out in *The Interim Director*, "It's much easier for an interim director to argue with a board than it is for a senior employee or even in some cases a full-time director." The reason for this is an interim's focus on delivering client value rather than protecting his or her career. It is also possible that an interim will move into new geographical settings, where their skills will be stretched even further. This will strengthen their courage and confidence.

. . . .

An interim is typically self-assured. This is not just an innate personality trait, but a result of a successful track record.

. . . .

The following example shows with clear definition some of the difficult decisions that an interim is confident making while undertaking a project.

Impact Example: Managing a delicate conflict of interest

> *In this assignment, an interim leader had to re-negotiate an outsourcing contractual relationship that had been in place for many years. As the interim began his analysis to establish a new contract that would deliver value for the client, it became clear that there was more to sift through than just commercial terms. The outsourcing firm had a complicated legal relationship with the client and there were outstanding questions about payment being made for services not provided, as well as more complex financial irregularities. There was a very delicate conflict of interest between the two organizations. The interim leader decided to pursue revisions to this contract with integrity and determination. While significant progress was made, the interim was eventually asked to focus on other projects without resolution to the outsourcing contract. It was later determined that the interim had turned over too many sensitive stones; this intervention threatened a commercial arrangement that would have resulted in money-laundering legal challenges in*

most countries. Courage to do what is right and
acknowledge the boundaries of engagement are
significant for an interim.

From the first contact with an effective interim leader, clients realize that they are engaging a professional with a vast amount of self-assurance, savvy, and capability. An interim is determined to make an impact for clients, stakeholders, and colleagues. This drive to make an impact is one of the most critical elements of success for an interim leader. Making an impact is at the root of an interim's motivation and it often reflects positively, after an interim intervention, on the bottom line of client organizations.

Case Study: Business Turnaround

How does an interim leader delve into the core workings of an organization to deliver an impact that makes a significant difference?

1. **Client Context**
The client is a leading supplier of small-scale clean energy recovery from waste plants and technology. Their technology provides a robust, local solution for the treatment of residual waste, by converting it into renewable energy which can then be used to provide local communities with heat and power. Their plants convert the waste into heat and /or electricity, using patented gasification technology. They have several plants in operation across Europe. Annual revenue £30m. Number of employees 90.

2. **Interim Assignment**
Turnaround from a technology development company to a project delivery company.

Some of the major challenges included:

- No coordination of the activities on site and no integrated programme; this created major delays on the project with no recognition that the civil engineering program being followed created significant overall delays to the project.
- The relationships between the client, contractor, and vendor were strained.
- There had been no change to the balance-sheet position, yet the company signed three additional projects, carrying the full risk associated with fixed budgets, cost overruns, and delays.
- The company had limited capability from the project risk and contingency funds that had been built into the project budget. Its capability to meet its obligations for any overruns or delays was also very limited.
- Contract milestone payments and company cash flow meant that, provided that the company continued to grow quickly and continue to secure orders, finances would not be a problem. It became apparent that no further orders were likely to be received in the coming two years.
- There was no consideration of cost by the design team as they were not accountable for the costs. The net result was a complete overdesign of many items.
- There was no central control of costs by the project manager and no control of procurement.
- There was a complete lack of understanding of the competence and capabilities of the original process owners; this had led to a complete breakdown of communication control and commitment of the original process owners.

3. Results

Business turnaround results, based on the interim's leadership and strategy, included:

- The interim immediately appointed commercial managers to each of the projects in order to get a handle on each of the project's finances and the likely outturn and cash requirements.
- Change of structure and change of management
- The interim negotiated with customers and banks regarding payments and overall financial position.
- Creation of a standardized plant design for a single line; this design was replicated for different size plants.
- Licensed the technology in China and set up discussions with the largest waste company in China and the owner of the national waste company in Poland.
- All the key staff were offered new employment in a new company and the technology was transferred into this new business.
- The new company would pursue the initiative with the Chinese and look to negotiate new service contracts on the existing plants under construction.
- The goal to have a service-based contract with no liabilities on cost or delays was met.

4. Benefits of an Interim Leader Solution

The following examples illustrate overall benefits of the appointment of an interim as well as benefits specific to this case study:

- An interim experienced in working under time pressures to get a company on the right track does not shy away from this type of challenge and is usually over qualified;

this interim has been in these situations before. This interim has the experience of knowing exactly what to do in such situations.

- For an experienced interim, there is no sentimentality or emotion associated with making the right decisions in a timely manner as the situation demands. In this case, the interim is continually working in the interest of the shareholder with total confidentiality as to the shareholder's intent, as this may conflict with the management of the business.

- An interim can assess a company's position and lay out the options for the shareholder very quickly. He or she is not there for a long-term career or as a fee earner, but to do the right thing for the shareholder. In circumstances like this, the shareholder ventured into new territory and the interim was able to advise the shareholder of the options in an impartial way.

CHAPTER 8

Leadership

Leadership – the capacity, influence, and ability to guide individuals, teams, or entire organizations

An interim leads organizations, teams, and individuals. He or she does not have an agenda, points to prove, a corporate career to advance, political battles to win (although an interim might do this), or people to impress. Interim leadership at its best displays a raw, spirited, purposeful, and focused intent.

Interim leadership at its best displays a raw, spirited, purposeful, and focused intent.

A chapter on leadership might appear obvious when discussing interim leadership. However, the fact that an interim is both a "leader" and a "specialist", warrants a closer look. Not only is an interim a specialist in their field of expertise, but he or she brings extensive leadership capability to develop and influence solutions that move organizations forward.

The interim mindset –to exceed client expectations —demands a high degree of motivation and direction. Indeed, an interim leader is self-led and self-propelled. This is part of the interim's DNA. Personal proficiency lies at the heart of the leadership model, according to Ulrich, Smallwood and Sweetman. In *The Leadership Code* they suggest, "Leaders who demonstrate personal proficiency follow rules about developing and increasing personal insight so that they model the change they want to see in others." This is what makes an interim so effective when tackling diverse organizational challenges that are complicated by a plethora of different relationships. An interim is a self-motivated, high-energy leader, and has a strong ethos to benefit everyone he or she engages.

All the SCILL Model© attributes complement and enhance each other, so it is no surprise that an interim's relational savvy makes him or her an effective leader. Underpinning this is the significant emotional intelligence that an interim develops, arising from the diversity of organizations and clients he or she collaborates with and leads. In *Primal Leadership* Goleman, Boyatzis and McKee unpack "primal leadership (original and most important)" when they state, "The key to making primal leadership work to everyone's advantage, lies in the leadership competencies of emotional intelligence; how leaders handle themselves and their relationships".

Not only is an interim an authentic and effective resource, he or she also has profound insight about themselves and others, gained through extensive professional experience; this makes an interim a well-rounded, effective leader. An interim provides phenomenal leadership in a distinct way; the choice of an interim career means that the interim has developed as a leader in multiple situations under unusual pressures. It is important for clients to understand the leadership portfolio an interim brings to any given situation and how this distinctive skill set can be leveraged.

In any organization, a mix of permanent leaders, consulting support, and the occasional burst of interim energy and acceleration makes for a potent leadership mix. Clients who choose not to include the potential impact of an interim leader miss the experience, gravitas, dynamism, and synergy –a significant value added —this individual brings when he or she connects with organizations.

How does an interim lead?

- Personal
- Situational
- Transformational
- Inspirational
- Reputational

Personal Leadership

One of the most important drivers behind organizational effectiveness is "leadership". This is why organizations are so careful to resource, develop, and retain the best leaders. Successful leaders make the difference. They create winning strategies, develop inspiring cultures, deliver optimum results, and motivate others. The best leaders carry a premium, and in most organizations, they rise to prominence.

Are there personal factors that make a leader great? Frequently, the difference between a "great" and "OK" leader is shaped by personal factors, such as a lifetime of experiences that have led to the growth of the leader, the role models he or she may have learned from, and the lessons learned. There is obviously an innate, genetic element to this as well, but the arguments of "born" or "made" are outside the scope of this discussion. Great leadership is arguably characterized by self-assurance, wisdom, vision, and an ability to engage the commitment of others. Most of these qualities are shaped throughout the lifetime of a leader. All accomplishments aside, it is often these personal attributes that distinguish a memorable leader.

What personal leadership qualities can a client expect from an interim leader?

- Self-assured
- Trustworthy
- Decisive
- Inspiring
- Adaptive
- Integrity
- Service-oriented
- Focused
- Results-oriented
- Humility

These and other leadership qualities are discussed in depth in Chapter 12 (GREAT Interim Competencies).

Most interims have held significant roles in organizations, many of them at the "C-Suite" level. Some have already had a tremendously successful career and are now giving back. Some interims are in early career stages but have realized that his or her best contribution to organizations is as an interim leader, for many of the reasons cited in earlier chapters. These leaders do not need an organizational "wrapper" to feel secure or effective. Neither is the interim content to dip in and out of organizations on consulting projects. What motivates an interim leader? The opportunity to lead organizations through times of transition, design and deliver new solutions, teams, processes, and implement these changes. An interim is often highly invested in the contribution for which he or she is responsible. In some ways, this level of commitment is more intense than if the interim is a permanent employee. There are many reasons for this. An interim leader has tremendous pride in his or her professional credibility, often demonstrated by the results the interim delivers and the positive impact he or she has on leaders and teams. Because his or her tenure is temporary, an interim gives one-hundred percent, and knows there is a fixed window in which to make an impact.

· ·

An interim gives one-hundred percent and knows there is a fixed window in which to make an impact.

· ·

An interim shows leadership before the start of an assignment. An interim takes the initiative to be active in networking, client business/industry research, project focused reading, and self-development. For example, prior to connecting with a client, an interim conducts background analysis to be prepared with ideas already germinating. Basically, an interim doesn't need an external motivator—the interim is self-motivated. Clients can trust an interim leader to assume leadership from day one of the assignment; this "take-charge" energy quickly becomes evident and inspires everyone around the interim. An interim's personal leadership is decisive, inspiring, and purposeful.

An interim leader often has an affinity with the "Level 5 leadership" defined by Jim Collins in *Good to Great*: "Fanatically driven, infected with an incurable need to produce results." Because an interim delivers results based on expertise, track-record, and high-performance interventions, he or she also has an affinity with the first virtue that Collins includes in his overall definition of Level 5 leadership: "An individual who blends extreme personal humility with intense professional will." An interim leader does not have anything to prove but takes pride in the ability to prove his or her worth.

Situational Leadership

One of the most powerful characteristics of an interim leader is adaptability. An interim is incredibly adaptive to the situations he or she experiences with clients and their organizations. Goffee and Jones describe this in *Why Should Anyone Be Led by You* as: "situation sensing – a mixture of sensory and cognitive abilities" and state, "Effective leaders tune into the organizational frequency to understand what is going on beneath the surface." This is described as "savvy" in Chapter 5 and shows how an interim is often highly skilled at sniffing out the root causes of issues and bringing effective solutions to a client.

An interim's CV presents, over time, a journey to many diverse organizations, often across different industry sectors, and with challenges that vary quite considerably. Leaders who understand the value of an interim leader recognize this agility and application as a major reason an interim is such an asset, rather than a questionable job-hopper. The diversity of an interim's experience gives the interim breadth and depth, including broad experience and significant situational awareness. Sometimes organizational leaders hesitate to employ those who have not had experience within their industry sector. However, sector is less important than success. If a leader has the core capabilities and track-record of delivery, then he or she is likely to repeat this success, regardless of the sector. For an interim, this track-record of delivery is the strength on which he or she is assessed. An interim's ability to leverage significant experience and skills – as the SCILL Model© suggests —across diverse organizations, distinguishes an interim from other leaders. This situational adaptability is one of the core leadership strengths that an interim brings to clients.

During many years of being an interim, the author has worked in a wide range of industry sectors including: finance, consumer goods, defense, energy, waste management, telecommunications, retail, professional services, and nonprofit. He has immersed himself in varied situations and assignments, including: joining a transformational team; leading an internal function; delivering significant projects; and leading the turnaround of critical activities. Such a diversity of assignments fuels an interim's motivation and provides a track record of adaptability, agility, and effectiveness—an interim delivers results for clients.

. . . .

A diversity of assignments fuels an interim's motivation and provides a track record of adaptability, agility, and effectiveness— an interim delivers results for clients.

. . . .

Whatever the challenge, an interim's experience and expertise as a leader across organizations means that his or her clients get significant value in one person, rather than the expense and potential headache of connecting with several different specialists who have niche experience. This is illustrated by the following example:

Leadership Example: Expanded leadership role offsets the specialist's lack of innovation

> *A client asked an interim leader to fulfil a leadership role for a specific workstream of a global outsourcing project. This role required interfacing with an outsourced consultancy who would provide the global solutions through a network of sub-vendors, as well as their own capabilities. This interface with the outsourced consultancy proved to be quite a challenge for the interim. The outsourced partner was asked to contribute a major element of innovation to the design of deliverables. To achieve this, the outsourced partner had to reach out to an innovation expert from another continent. This lack of immediate innovation in the proposals was surprising. The interim leader took a much larger leadership role in this aspect of the project, due to the outsourced partner's lack of expertise, agility, and innovation. The interim also had to take on the role of design authority for 120 different project elements because the quality and accuracy of the outsourced partner's stewardship were lacking. The interim leader's experience in this field was invaluable*

at a leadership and strategic level. The interim's attitude and commitment to attend to the level of detail required for success proved essential in ensuring that the client got the results expected. In some respects, the interim's results exceeded client expectations by making up for the lack of contribution by the outsourced partner.

An interim is unlikely to be swayed by contractual nuances when determining whether to take certain actions; as a decisive leader who quickly assesses the situation, an interim is more likely to seek forgiveness than to ask permission. The interim is also likely to raise issues and challenges that others might avoid, ensuring all parties step up to the level required for a successful outcome. In Blanchard and Hersey's Situational-Leadership-Model parlance, interim leaders are "High Competence / High Commitment" with an agility to flex across different levels of "Follower Readiness and Leadership Styles". What does this mean? An interim's high level of flexibility, competence, and commitment makes him or her a high-value asset who delivers specific value for a specific purpose over a specific timeline.

Transformational Leadership

Leading change is an interim's strength. As Chapter 10 (Interims and Change) explores in more detail, an interim leader is a skillful navigator of change, especially when the context is a crisis, or a volatile situation and a speedy resolution is required. Of course, change is often a constant paradigm in many organizations, unless of course the existing leadership has led the organization down a blind alley!

There is a big business in change management –the strategy, processes, and planning. Equally in demand is change leadership. The client's strategy for change may be ready, but the employees– often this includes leaders—are not. Some leaders resist change, others war against it, others may fear it, and still others may be blind to it. How can an organization ensure that leaders are able to lead people through change? An interim leader has wide experience in a range of organizations and is adept at managing all aspects of change and transformation.

An interim leader thrives on change: leading into the unknown, anticipating and planning for change, and creating new ways of working. The characteristics of a leader to adapt, anticipate, and articulate change are without question essential leadership traits; this is especially true for an interim leader who must face challenges in a range of organizational cultures, skillfully plan strategy, build relationships, and deliver results under short time pressures.

Transformational change demands transformational leadership. Often leaders find themselves in circumstances where they are required to map out transformational change in their organizations. This can be triggered by market conditions, competitive challenges, geographical maneuvering, regulatory requirements, technology changes, and many other stimuli. The decision to hire an interim to lead transformational change is a wise one as the level of complexity can be exponential. Often, when an interim or client leadership define transformational programs, there are all sorts of other embedded transformations that make up the strategic plan. Navigating this requires the seasoned insight and experience that an interim brings. Consider the following example:

Leadership Example: Transformational expertise for organizations and people

> *A client asked an interim leader to use his expertise to further the client's ambitions by readying senior leadership for an exponential growth strategy. This was launched by a significant leadership conference which the interim leader was asked to design, plan, and facilitate. The conference was a great success. This was followed by work assignments covering organizational design, board evaluation, leadership profiling and coaching, performance-system overhaul, mentoring-program design, and developing key processes for management. Organizations are complex systems. And not just that, they are filled with people! The interim's ability to bring transformational expertise to the ways that organizations work, as well as his deep experience of the people dynamics of transformation, proved essential.*

What is the difference an interim leader brings to organizational transformation? An interim has battle scars from the experience of leading people amidst the dynamics of change in complex organizations. An interim brings experiential learning and uses a vibrant imagination to create innovative solutions. An interim is comfortable, even welcomes, being asked to lead the line when it comes to transformation. This contrasts with permanent leaders, who often seek to build the organization in a systemic way and to build resourcing models that will support this over the long term. This also contrast with consultancies, who bring their organizational machinery with them and often have intelligent resources without having the cultural insight and savvy described in Chapter 5 (Savvy). There is a place for permanent leaders and consultancies as well as interims in the process of transformation. To assist client organizations in choosing the best resource, these differences are explored in more detail in Chapter 1 (Why Interim Leaders?).

. . . .

An interim brings experiential learning and uses a vibrant imagination to create innovative solutions.

. . . .

There is a case for considering change management as the norm, a best practice, of excellent leadership. An interim's bread and butter behavior is to be a transformational leader. An interim is inspired to make a difference, see others empowered in new ways, and help organizations on the upward curve of change.

Inspirational Leadership

Having an interim in the ranks is inspirational for all concerned. The interim leader brings a dynamism, wisdom, and confidence that is immediately apparent. This is reassuring for the leadership who hired the interim and a boost to staff — an extremely capable leader and colleague just joined the team.

An interim inspires leaders in the organization to show that the return on their interim-investment adds significant value. This value is not always immediately measurable, but most would agree that the presence of an interim motivates and enhances the performance of the whole team. The interim is an experienced, change-oriented, and high-profile leader who brings energy, inspiration, and confidence to others.

. . . .

The presence of a dynamic, change-oriented, and high-profile expert brings energy, inspiration, and confidence to others.

. . . .

By the very nature of their experience, drive, and talent, interims inject inspiration to teams and organizations. This can have some strange side-effects. For example, some clients can be reluctant to expose an interim to senior leadership. This might be because the interim leader is more inspirational than the permanent leaders and the immediate client leader feels over-shadowed by the interim's gravitas and ideas. It may be that the interim is regarded as a contract resource, and therefore not to be included at the leadership table; in this case, the organization's leadership fails to recognize the interim's value, and the fact that the interim is an equal who has held roles as influential as those held by many of the permanent leaders. Leaders can be personally, politically, professionally, or culturally motivated when it comes to being jealous of an interim's inspirational leadership and contributions. An interim offers timely insights, observations, and effective proposals to deliver results. Indeed, it could be said that an interim's provocation of norms is quite acute. The interim needs to ensure that this is done in a balanced way, by offering insights with objective and well-researched arguments, and to avoid being critical of the organization or making recommendations without collaboration. An effective leader is strategic and savvy, using the talents of others to his or her advantage and playing the collegiate and team game to complement the advancement of his or her own role. The following serves as an interesting example:

Leadership Example: Inspiring a shift from SME to leadership peer

An interim leader was working with a client on a critical project related to the pipeline of future business owners. The client was enthusiastic about having the interim add Subject-Matter-Expert value but was reluctant for him to meet with senior leaders without being accompanied. Over a period of many months the client's position softened and the interim leader was able to proactively connect with senior leaders as needed. In fact, there were some occasions where the key client was unable to attend certain meetings and the interim attended as interaction with senior leaders was essential. The reputation and judgement of the interim impressed senior leadership to the point where they saw the interim as a peer and equal of the permanent client leader, rather than a hired hand.

An interim's ability to inspire is especially evident among existing team members. Clients may ask an interim to lead others, or alternatively just ask the interim to deliver a project only as the Subject Matter Expert. Leading other resources, whether internal or contract, is an opportunity for an interim to display high-class leadership.

How does an interim's leadership inspire a team and boost morale?

- great coaching
- clear planning
- timely communication
- regular motivation

- change in pace of delivery

The opportunity for an interim to impact the team's motivation, atmosphere, and climate is immense. The team may have come off the back of a difficult leader, been leaderless for a while, or may have relationship issues that need addressing. An interim can do wonders for individuals and an organization with inspirational leadership that transforms teams and individuals —and delivers excellent projects and results.

An interim leader also inspires colleagues by modeling leadership in the way that the interim assignment is executed.

How does an interim's leadership of an assignment inspire the team?

- effective project management disciplines
- upgrading communications
- applying change management techniques
- bringing clarity to stakeholders
- engaging experts
- being visible, the evident project leader

Demonstrating leadership in visible, tangible ways, such as the simple act of taking a marker and mapping strategy on the whiteboard, inspires teams; client leadership and teams observe an inspirational interim leader who has focus and direction. Filling this leadership role with energy and dynamism is standard best practice for an interim. An interim leader is a master of the art of leadership, and brings confident opinions, bold positioning, and the savvy determination to ensure that each contributing resource delivers value to the success of the project.

. . . .

An interim leader is a master of the art of leadership, and brings confident opinions, bold positioning, and the savvy determination to ensure that each contributing resource delivers value to the success of the project.

. . . .

Reputational Leadership

An interim leader takes pride in enhancing the reputation of others and the organizations with which he or she is associated. An interim's investment in colleagues, partnerships, and projects brings positive dividends to the internal leaders. It's almost as though the interim gets a buzz from the way his or her "shine" rubs off on others as the organization become more successful, partially resulting from the interim's hard work. Often, an interim leader will associate a sense of "family" and "collegiate pride" with clients and projects. Not surprisingly, an interim leader typically maintains contact with previous clients and cares deeply about the success of the individuals and careers impacted by his or her contributions.

An interim leader builds a portfolio of client engagements—this is the interim's most important marketing tool —second only to the person, the individual interim. In fact, this portfolio is highly significant for an interim's reputation, given that the interim role is one of leadership, not just service delivery. Being known as a leader who brings gravitas, energy, and results is the business card of an interim leader.

. . . .

Being known as a leader who brings gravitas, energy, and results is the business card of an interim leader.

. . . .

How does an interim enhance his or her personal reputation? An interim leads himself (or herself) by building an outstanding reputation for the added value brought to clients. It is rare that an interim has an assignment or client experience that is not a resounding success. An interim is a smart, experienced, and sometimes outspoken individual who has a significant contribution to add. An interim leader cares intensely about the reputation that he or she builds with the client. An interim's contribution is never a "fire-and-forget" project, but rather something the interim hopes brings enhanced value and performance to the client.

An interim leader is driven to build a second-to-none reputation with a client portfolio of results and achievements. An interim is proud to be considered by clients and peers as among the best in the leadership field. It is this drive for reputational leadership—to exceed expectations on all levels—that ensures the interim is of the highest value to prospective clients.

Case Study: Systems Upgrade

How might an interim leader be required to step into line leadership responsibilities to deliver significant strategic value to the client?

1. **Client Context**
UK-based, retail financial services organization, with 300 stores, annual revenue of £350m, and 3,000 employees. Private equity owned.

2. **Assignment**
Line leadership of the IT function for 14 months, following the unanticipated departure of the Chief Information Officer, to

provide a new strategic direction prior to the appointment of a permanent staff member.

This assignment demanded a close relationship integration with and influencing of the client's leadership team; the objective was to shape strategies to optimize the customer offer while also driving operational efficiencies.

Executive priorities included:

- Satisfy the requirements of the industry regulator
- Grow revenue
- Closely manage financial risk
- Maximize enterprise value in readiness for a future equity transaction

3. **Results**

The client was pleased with the outcomes of the assignment; the interim achieved these by replicating best-practice experience that he gained in large, more complex environments. Specific achievements included:

- The interim led the extension and execution of the company's e-commerce strategy, in partnership with the marketing director, resulting in 20% of new business originating from Internet sales leads.
- The interim revised the IT strategy to focus on a new enterprise-resource planning platform. This included selecting a supplier, building the business case and gaining executive approval for a £multi-million investment to yield cost savings. More importantly, the interim provided long-term organizational scalability.
- The interim turned around the reputation of the IT function

through a renewed focus on internal customer satisfaction, zero tolerance for software defects, and by delivering multiple upgrades to make life easier for store staff. This included, for example, reducing in-store transaction times by 50%.

- The introduction of a formal change-governance approach helped to balance available resources across multiple crucial programs.
- The interim developed a supply strategy for IT and telecoms, delivering material savings within the £multi-million annual budget through low-risk commercial intervention and by introducing proven alternative solutions.
- A thorough human resource review of the 40 members of the IT team yielded a planned turnover of low performers and greater contributions from other staff.

4. Benefits of an Interim Leader Solution

The key benefit of hiring the interim leader: Access to a higher-level of expertise and experience than the client would typically find in similar, permanent staff-member roles. In this case, this meant that the interim leader was confident of success, which in turn ensured the confidence of the client company's leadership. The interim leader had experience in larger, more complex environments and would not have considered the client as a potential employer if he had been searching for a permanent role.

Other important benefits include:
- The immediate availability of the interim leader.
- The near break-even cost-comparison of the interim route versus using an equivalent permanent staff member.
- The flexibility of the interim leader to work on a part-time basis when exiting the client company, enabling a clean departure with a thorough knowledge transfer.

CHAPTER 9

Legacy

Legacy – something handed down from one generation to the next that often continues to exist

This chapter builds on the reputational leadership discussion in Chapter 8 to demonstrate a core driver of an interim leader. Since an interim seeks to build a portfolio of success throughout his or her career, leaving a legacy is important. For many permanent leaders, a legacy in the world of work means long service, awards, and an honorable send-off to retirement. An interim leader also finds value in leaving a legacy. As Jim Collins states in *Good to Great*, "It is very difficult to have a meaningful life without meaningful work." Meaningful work is what an interim craves, and an interim often leaves a series of legacies to organizations, projects, and people that are a testament to a productive career.

Each client engagement offers an interim leader an opportunity to make an impact, effect critical change, transition an organization, and inspire staff. Each time an interim starts a contract, he or she often already knows what legacy to leave. An interim is not working for glory or awards, but instead works to enhance the client organization and its employees. Like any leader, an interim takes great pride in delivering successful results that attest to his or her professional and personal contribution. An interim has a driving force to tackle a challenge and if possible, to overachieve in his or her short time with the client organization. As Alasdair Drysdale notes in *The Interim Director*, "Make sure that when you finish your project(s) your client has all the tools and skills needed to continue successfully from where you have finished." Not only does an interim deliver against assigned accountabilities, the interim also leaves clients with continuity that stems from his or her contributions.

• •

An interim has a driving force to tackle a challenge and if possible, overachieve in his or her short time with the client organization.

• •

When professionals write their CV's, one of the most common challenges is to identify achievements that have measurable value. For an interim, this should be easy. When an interim leader produces his or her CV, it is easier to point to specific achievements, results, and leadership than it might be for a long-term employee who often has to sift through many other accountabilities to build a punchy CV. Focusing on results is an interim's chief goal. A client hires an interim to deliver specific value-associated projects with a specific scope of work. If an assignment isn't defined with specific metrics, one of an interim's first go-to tasks is to define them. It is not enough to make a contribution that is measured in good feelings, positive accolades, and warm gestures. The interim mindset is to exceed client expectations. An interim leader is driven by achievement and the delivery of results. One of an interim's rewards is to review his or her CV, full of legacies to organizations and projects where the interim made an impact, and to the leaders and teams who benefited.

. . . .
The interim mindset is to exceed client expectations.
. . . .

Who benefits from an interim's legacy?

- Organizations
- Projects
- People

Organizations

Clients often cite "a fresh pair of eyes" as one of the greatest benefits of hiring an interim. And not just any eyes— experienced and insightful eyes! Whether it is during a merger or acquisition, a transformational program, or a strategic project, most clients expect an interim to make observations and contributions at a macro level as well as on specific assignments. Why? Because one of an interim's key skills is to systemically survey an organization's environment. An interim brings insight into networks, relationships, hierarchy, spans of control, decision-making tree, roles and responsibilities, and many other aspects of an organization's culture and infrastructure.

The interim mindset is to leave the organization in a better place than when the interim joined it. As Alasdair Drysdale suggests in *The Interim Director*, "If you see that the business is not going to obtain the full benefits of your work because of some inadequacy elsewhere, you must make sure that that inadequacy is rectified during your time with the client." For example, if a client does not ask an interim to make observations on organizational design in addition to other project deliverables, the interim will take the initiative to make recommendations anyway.

Consider the following examples of interim assignments:

Legacy Example: Organizing leadership roles for an engineering academy

1. *An interim leader was referred to a client to transform the operation of an engineering academy, primarily from a strategic learning perspective. Apart from the technological, legislative, and commercial focus, probably the greatest legacy the interim would leave was the organization of the academy. The team who had been leading the academy were all great professionals. Their roles, however, were quite muddled. It was essential to step back and assess the functions the academy needed to perform, the representation that this required at a leadership level, and who was in those roles or could be brought in to supplement or replace them. The interim went on to formalize roles, create new ones, and brought discipline to the way the organization operated. This served to provide a more effective framework in which to deliver solutions for the other aspects of the assignment.*

Legacy Example: Reorganizing a project team with an increasing volume of work

> 2. *This client had a problem that is not uncommon in most organizations: the project environment was growing every year. It was slowly killing the team members who were straining under the burden of more and more work without a change in team structure. During a team review, the client leader asked, "What changes would you like to see in the team if you came back after a year of being away?" Most team members offered tactical suggestions, probably because their daily lives were spent fighting fires and addressing the next task in front of them. The interim leader's observation was a complete realignment of the team designed to deliver clarity, efficiency, and future-proofing. This suggestion took a while to take root, but a year later a realignment was implemented that looked a lot like the suggestion the interim had made.*

An interim leader has a distinctive ability to build legacies that impact organizations more deeply than the scope of an interim's projects. An interim's judgment and recommendations carry a high degree of objectivity, and senior leaders do well to absorb an interim's insight. An interim's clarity and foresight aren't muddled by the melee of day-to-day operations, and his or her savvy enables an interim to grasp the context of recommendations with a high degree of accuracy.

An interim's chosen career path of building expertise with many organizations over a span of multiple contracts is a very effective way of bringing leadership wisdom into organizations. An interim leader not only has a responsibility to deliver account-abilities, but also to help organizations chart a course through the challenges and opportunities that lie ahead. Helping leaders and teams see a new paradigm requires more than presenting a new vision. It requires a reasoned, cognitive, and commercial discussion before any emotional or aspirational leaps can be made. This is where the experience of an interim can help transition thinking and lead organizations into exciting new places. As McGovern and Russell state in *A New Brand of Expertise*, "Proven interims are highly prized individuals who consistently provide value to companies far in excess of their costs." This is an essential interim leadership legacy.

. . . .

An interim leader is an increasingly effective way of injecting leadership wisdom into an organization.

. . . .

Projects

Leaving a legacy of an effectively delivered project is immense-ly rewarding. It is often sobering for an interim leader to reflect on his or her work and its impact on thousands of employees — often the whole organization – many times over. The nature of interim projects is such that they are often strategic, transforma-tional, and far-reaching. Indeed, many interims lead numerous projects that have been major organizational initiatives.

For some leaders, a legacy of "projects" might seem insubstan-tial, disjointed, or diverse. Yet much of organizational strategy and operation is split into projects – even when these proj-ects last numerous years. It is the nature of a leader who has chosen an interim leader career to be driven by the need to deliver something—a project—that is tangible and significant, and to do this over and over again. An interim's legacy can fill many pages and illustrates diversity, delivery, and dedication. Sometimes an interim is required to deliver solutions and then hand them over to others for implementation. This can be stimulating in the sense that the next project for a new client might require another burst of ingenuity and energy. It can also be frustrating; by the time a project lands and has an impact the interim leader might not see or experience it first-hand. An interim needs to work within this dynamic, i.e., lead either design and delivery without implementation, or with the latter as part of the assignment.

There are some disciplines that transcend employment type; delivering projects against objectives within the parameters of time, cost, and quality is one of them. Drifting through day-to-day tasks might be the experience of some individuals and maybe some organizations, but it is certainly not the domain of an interim. One of the legacies that an interim delivers to an organization is a discipline in the way that projects are conducted. An interim conducts a project with detailed, strategic attention to planning, resources, dependencies, contingencies, and cost. An effective interim builds a coherent framework in which to deliver – and exceed —the client's expectations. This often includes developing, and in some cases, executing plans for change, resourcing, communications, and engagement. The disciplines of operating as an interim are discussed further in the Chapter 15.

Most interim leaders are incredibly proud of the projects they have delivered. Some of these might be within formal project frameworks, some within the context of targets needing to be met, and others are business imperatives that need concentration and fortitude to make them happen. Whatever the definition of a project, an interim leader contributes substantially to the most significant ones in an organization. For an interim, delivering projects is a day-to-day reality that yields long-term rewards. Clearly, the legacy of delivering impactful project results within limited timeframes motivates an interim. An interim leader is motivated to achieve, committed to deliver, and passionate about success.

. . . .

An interim leader is motivated to achieve, committed to deliver, and passionate about success.

. . . .

People

Possibly the most important legacy that an interim leaves is with the people in the client organization. Despite the passage of time and career changes, many interim leaders maintain relationships with the colleagues with whom he or she has worked. And yet the driving force for an interim is not necessarily to build life-long relationships, but to build many significant relationships that provide value for all stakeholders. An interim leader's legacy is to forge relationships around his or her significant contributions and impact.

Unlike many consulting engagements, an interim assignment means that an interim leader is often asked to take on accountability for internal teams for the duration of the assignment. This might be to achieve the delivery of a project, accomplish a turnaround, or simply to provide leadership pending a permanent appointment. The following examples illustrate how an interim leader can impact personal relationships:

Legacy Example: Developing career goals for a mismatched employee

1. *Joe was the director of sales in a client organization in which an interim leader was working to implement a corporate change program. As often happens with interims, their experience and stature are called upon to help leaders in organizations in ways that are beyond the scope of the project on which they are working; this of course includes coaching and mentoring. Joe's challenge was a significant career choice that he was considering. His driving ambition was to run his own sales company, and yet he found himself in a corporate environment that he was not thrilled about. During a period of months, the interim coached him through his motivations, capabilities, and choices. One day, Joe resigned in order to set up his own sales organization with a partner. This is a great result and legacy – a distracted employee gained the motivation to begin a new career and the organization had a chance to bring in a new team member into a role that demanded significant focus.*

Legacy Example: Promoting a diamond-in-the-rough

2. *The interim leader was asked to build a center of excellence within a client organization; this required re-organization as well as additional resourcing. The interim prided himself on being a good judge of people and interviewed Trevor for a role on the team. He was a diamond-in-the-rough, he was under-qualified, had patchy experience, and yet showed drive, tenacity, and intelligence that left a good impression. The interim*

leader decided to offer him the role. Over the next few months, Trevor impressed everyone with his accomplishments. When the interim's contract concluded, Trevor was quickly promoted to be the Head of Function and performed admirably in that role. Over the years, Trevor applied himself to this new role, furthered his education, and developed a subsequent career in consulting. Part of the interim's legacy in working with this client was his interaction with Trevor; the interim leader identified Trevor's raw talent and gave him a career opportunity that will benefit him for years to come.

An interim is motivated by the results that he or she delivers and the people with whom he or she collaborates. Leaving behind a trail of empowered, motivated, and focused individuals is perhaps more important than any other legacy an interim leaves. An interim leader looks at his or her career as an opportunity to mark-up big wins within short-time periods across a diverse range of clients. The reward is not a gold clock on the twenty-fifth anniversary of employment, but rather a track-record of achievements, satisfied clients, and relationships forged in the fires of critical challenges.

Case Study: Revitalize Integrated Business & HR Strategy & Culture Change Program

How is an interim leader's legacy more than just project deliverables? As this case study illustrates, an interim's legacy encompasses deep strategic and cultural changes that impact the character and direction of organizations.

---

1. Client Context

Highly acquisitive privately owned Fast Moving Consumer Goods business, £3.2bn turnover, predominantly UK based, covering 45 locations and employing 23,00 colleagues. The interim's initial nine-month contract was extended to 18 months.

2. Assignment

The Interim was hired as Group People & Change Director to address:

- Business strategy, organization structure, and future capability requirements
- People strategy, post-acquisition "recovery", and fit for future
- Culture change and leadership behaviors of top 150 leaders

3. Results
- As a board member, the interim:
  - o Jointly formulated medium-term business strategy, a three-year plan (including a range of change in ownership options),
  - o Recruited two additional non-executive directors (satisfying bond-holder requirements), introduced (and hired) for the new role of COO,

---

- o Re-designed top-team structure to free up CEO resource,
- o Provided greater organizational and role clarity at Group level,
- o Secondary exercise included to then identify top-team succession plan and capability gaps for subsequent action.
- The interim re-built and re-energized the Group HR function following the removal of two previous Divisional HRDs and associated "blockers". This included:
  - o Identified, developed, and promoted previously hidden HR talent as "change champions",
  - o Delivered reduction of £3m in HR overhead, including transition to Recruitment Process Outsourcing recruitment model with 50% YoY savings,
  - o Specified, hired, and on-boarded permanent Group People & Change Director, including two-month handover before departure (another key learning for successful transition).
- As the Board's champion, the interim:
  - o introduced a cultural change initiative program via the Annual Top 150 leaders conference (culture metrics increased by 50% YoY),
  - o introduced the first ever Group-wide leadership development three-day workshops. These were grounded in psychometric behavioural insights, team learning, and individual-action planning, all linked to annually measured employee engagement scores across each of the 45 locations. (Voluntary take-up of 95% from the 150 business leaders).

4. **Benefits of an Interim Solution**

The use of an experienced interim provided the organization with the needed culture change catalyst; this interim is a strategic and highly pragmatic, commercially-minded people leader; this interim worked also as the in-house top-team coach; and is the "previously tried, trusted, and tested agent provocateur" that the Board believed they needed.

An interim leader needs to be constantly aware of and manage the potential conflict inherent in an interim appointment. An interim is hired to have an immediate impact, to "hit the ground running", to bring all the years of skill, knowledge and experience to the client's business. Yet, for an interim, there is no future in the organization; an interim is careful to avoid creating a relationship of "personal dependency". Instead, an interim leader creates a legacy of interventions which others, often new board hires, will build upon to even greater success. An interim who is not comfortable with passing the torch, so to speak, may not flourish amidst the potential conflict of "interim vs. permanent" leadership and needs to consider whether being an interim is the right career.

PART III

The Value of Interim Leaders

CHAPTER 10

Interims and Change

"Effective executives treat change as an opportunity rather than a threat."

— Peter Drucker, *The Effective Executive*

Change keeps organizations vibrant and relevant. Two essential aspects of change, innovation and creativity, are fundamental to interim leadership. In *The Forgotten Half of Change*, Luc De Brabandere defines innovation as, "The approach whereby a team manages to change reality. Creativity is how an individual succeeds in changing his or her perception." An interim leader leans into innovation and creativity with a strong commitment. An interim effectively leads organizational and individual change, whether the change requires the innovation of teams, or the contribution of a creative individual.

. . . .
An interim leader leans into innovation and creativity with a strong commitment.
. . . .

While Part II of this book unpacked the DNA of an interim leader, based on the SCILL Model©, Part III digs deeper into the three elements that shape an interim's value and effectiveness: Change, Coach, and Competencies. This chapter explores the benefits of interim interventions and facets of change led by the introduction of an experienced, dynamic professional in a key temporary role.

Why is change leadership a primary focus when assessing leadership effectiveness, and developing and selecting leaders? In *Built To Last,* Collins and Porras discuss the concept of alignment; in their view, companies transform themselves into visionary companies through two key alignment processes:

1) developing new alignments to preserve the core and stimulate progress
2) eliminating misalignments that drive an organization away from its core ideology and those that impede progress toward the envisioned future

Both alignment and misalignment considerations are fertile ground for an interim leader; areas of insightful capability. The Confederation of British Industry states in their business guide, *Interim Executive Management,* "Interims are hungry for the challenge of changing the state of things and know they can do it because they have successfully done so on many occasions."

Change, or transition, is not only an area of deep capability for an interim leader, it is an area of significant comfort. An interim understands change perhaps more than most leaders because of the interim's repeated confrontations with it on the front line. An interim leader understands change and delivers the results required at all levels—organizational, process, and emotional. As Bridges states in *Managing Transitions,* "The first task of change management is to understand the destination and how to get there, the first task of transition management is to convince people to leave home." Interim leaders are skilled in both challenges.

How does an interim add value through his or her leadership in this area of organizational development? An interim's affinity for leading change illustrates how he or she is a positive catalyst for organizations that need help delivering a transition. In the context of interim leadership, there are several dynamics that impact an interim's ability to lead change:

- Scope of Change
- Politics of Change
- Speed of Change
- Communication of Change
- Embedding Change

Scope of Change

Interim assignments are most effective when they are focused and the primary objective and scope of the project or intervention is clearly defined. In these cases, the match of the resourcing solution (the right interim leader) to the organizational need is also well defined. At the other end of the spectrum, an interim can help create the necessary shape and definition of an interim assignment.

Three aspects of change assignments illustrate the context in which an interim leader can prove his or her effectiveness:

a) Broad

When a business leader needs assistance defining strategy and championing its adoption, an interim is an ideal solution. Not only does an interim bring the benefit of wide, panoramic experience, but he or she also brings the ability to engage quickly at a strategic level with both content and stakeholders.

In these instances, an interim enjoys the freedom of definition and creativity more than if the assignment was concise in nature. The challenges, however, are many. For example, broad definition of a change opportunity is more difficult for an organization to sponsor than a project that is defined and just needs launching. It is more challenging to define and "sell" a broad platform that hasn't been previously defined in-house, than it is to deliver a project that already has roots in the organization's strategy and on-going dialogue.

An interim engaged in a broad change opportunity works closely with internal leaders to ensure buy-in, collaboration, and visioning. The interim's skills, particularly in managing relationships, are essential, as well as the interim's ability to be strategic and connect the organization's past, present, and future.

. . . .

An interim has a strategic ability to connect the organization's past, present, and future.

. . . .

b) Incremental

It is not unusual for change projects to reproduce many subsequent projects. For example, an organization's culture change program will have a knock-off effect on its performance management infrastructure, compensation system, resourcing frameworks, development programs, and other systems.

An interim working on a defined project often sees this ripple-effect spread to other aspects of the organization. This spread of projects, or incremental change, may already be in motion when the interim arrives. This creates great opportunities for an interim who has both the skill set and inclination to broaden his or her involvement with a client.

An interim leader brings focus and dedication within an environment of incremental change. Rather than becoming an agitator or perpetuator of instability, an interim builds context and order to the change management plan and delivery requirements. The interim's presence in the organization is not merely to point out what needs to change and articulate alternative strategies. An interim shows business acumen and maturity to plot a course of change, prioritize activities, and lead programs and projects when asked. Clients and change committees quickly see an interim as an asset with valuable, objective perspectives, challenges, and ideas.

c) Defined

When a client asks an interim to deliver results within the scope of a well-defined change program, the interim's responsibilities are clear. The interim funnels energy and focus into this discrete area.

Clients can be tempted to stretch an interim's involvement to other activities that could be considered part of an overall change program, but it is important for the interim to channel attention to the immediate project and avoid "scope creep". One reason clients hire an interim is for this dedicated focus. An interim leader delivers results, without the constraints and distractions of organizational "noise" such as meetings and conflicts, that often slow the pace of development. Delivery is key! If an interim fails to deliver against the scope of a project, the cost of the interim is not justified. If, however, an interim is successful in delivering a defined change project, the client will take note and likely ask the interim to stretch his or her involvement elsewhere in the organization.

The topic of change is complex, and an interim operates in organizations where change is often messy rather than straightforward—hence, the prevalence of change management methodologies. Cameron and Green define organizations as organisms in *Making Sense of Change Management;* these organisms are "open, interconnected, interdependent subsystems." Within these organisms or organizations, Cameron and Greene describe effective change methodology as a way of designing interventions "to decrease resistance to change and increase the forces for change." Interim leaders are proven leaders of change — active proponents of methodologies that bring structure to the journey.

Understanding organizations and designing change interventions is second nature for an interim leader. Familiarity with change management methodologies helps an interim define the scope of change and plot a path forward. An interim should be cautious, however, to apply these methodologies in a way that is not mechanistic. For example, Kotter's Eight-Step Model needs context in the culture, sector, complexity, and maturity of the organization.

Politics of Change

In most organizations, politics play a significant role in change leadership. An interim observes politics in many ways; as an element of organizational culture and leadership team dynamics, a characteristic of fiefdoms, resistance, or union involvement, or just the way individual leaders operate. Of course, politics is not always a negative force. There are excellent reasons why change may need to be moderated, a direction reconsidered, or competing interests mediated. There may also be unexpected outcomes that arise from push-backs or alternative suggestions. In these instances, an interim remains professional, objective, and rational. The interim observes where the real power lies, who are the critical stakeholders, and what are the most effective influencing strategies.

It is essential that an interim be objective and not take sides. An interim faces the challenge of rising above endemic organizational politics to be a voice of reason, reconciliation, and reformation. As the Confederation of British Industry describes in their business guide, *Interim Executive Management*, an interim is "politically sensitive without being drawn into the politics, understands the need to stay objective and will not go 'native', particularly on an extended assignment."

. . . .

An interim rises above endemic organizational politics to be a voice of reason, reconciliation, and reformation.

. . . .

Since an interim has a short-term tenure with an organization, he or she has more liberty than a long-term employee to navigate and challenge political norms. An interim does this with an authentic interest in the organization's growth and the leaders' development. There are occasions when an interim gets caught up in the politics of an organization. For example, an interim may be drawn into confidential conversations that impact senior leaders, often because a leader seeks the interim's opinions on proposed actions. In these instances, an interim offers impartial, thoughtful input.

C-suite leaders are the key players in politics and most organizations have strong characters in these leadership roles. Indeed, some leaders earn reputations for being outspoken and hardcore. An effective interim responds to leadership cues with savvy and builds relationships with even the most feared and aloof leaders in organizations. An interim brings an objective voice of reason to a situation that might otherwise result in a polarized stand-off.

There are times when an interim is shielded from internal politics, or simply must turn a blind eye. For many an interim leader these are moments of relief. If an interim wanted politics on a daily basis, he or she would have chosen to be a permanent employee. However, an interim is often an adept political player given their experience, and he or she rises to the challenge of political maneuvering if required.

Speed of Change

As discussed previously in this book, the speed at which an interim is able to deliver results is a product of the interim's experience, confidence, and resilience. An interim prefers to be the agent of change, not the subject of change. Charles Handy, in *The Age of Unreason,* cites "discontinuous upside-down thinking" as the way a dynamic leader impacts our changing world. An interim leader loves to play in this sand-pit of chaos and change!

• •

An interim's raison d'être is to accelerate the pace of change.

• •

An interim's *raison d'être* is to accelerate the pace of change. If an interim is able to deliver on his or her accountabilities as part of organizational change then the interim will leave a legacy of value and transformation. If the interim encounters an organizational culture that is blocked by obstacles, whether the result of authorization hierarchies, budget, or other constraints, the interim's effectiveness and energy will lose momentum. The following example illustrates this:

EXAMPLE: Listening to cultural cues about changes in approach

> *A client asked an interim leader to offer a recom-mendation on how to develop the organization's leaders. The interim developed a comprehensive and experiential program, with a commitment of approximately five hours per month, to begin im-mediately. The client's response to this proposal was, "Thank you. But we've got some other ideas for this based around an existing curriculum of training courses and some other tried and tested methods." These client proposals were a con-tinuation of the existing slow and steady leader-ship development strategy, which had not had a dramatic impact, hence the request made of*

the interim for an alternative recommendation. Clearly, the client and the interim did not have a shared understanding or approach. While this was possible to resolve, this situation highlights how the organization's traditional and risk-averse culture dictated the investment, pace, and potential outcomes of any intervention.

When leading change an interim leader is usually steps ahead of others in their needs assessment and recommendation of solutions. An interim moves change at such a pace that he or she needs to slow down to engage permanent stakeholders. There are many reasons this may occur: the culture of the organization may be slow; leaders need to juggle other competing interests; or other stakeholders do not dedicate the time needed to maintain such a high pace. For an interim this demands patience and careful management. An interim can add value by working on subsidiary and supporting activities while stakeholders "catch up" to the interim's pace. In some cases, an interim may propose another task to be considered later in the project lifecycle – getting a jump on its execution while there is an opportunity.

Often when presenting clients with a direction of change an interim presents alternative scenarios. These might include scenarios in which the pace of change is fast compared with the status quo, and other scenarios with varying degrees of compromise. Clients often prefer choosing from a few options before finalizing a preferred way forward.

This process of providing clients with options also helps an interim achieve buy-in for proposed changes. This is especially important when an interim has to deliver change at a rapid pace;

one of an interim's greatest challenges is effectively engaging leaders and teams in this journey. An interim uses comprehensive stakeholder mapping to help engage support for change. An interim maps and determines diverse strategies to engage commitment from others. Of course, if senior leaders in the client organization are already leading change at a good pace, an interim simply needs to deliver against expectations, and has less need for mapping "buy-in" strategies; senior leadership is already on board. Speed of change is a familiar concept for an interim. An interim is not rattled when riding the change-curve roller coaster and is less disturbed when projects lurch in different directions. An interim's ability to react quickly and change course, even in the face of uncertainty and shifting horizons, is an essential part of the interim's tool kit as a change leader. An interim's ability to navigate change and feed off its energy leads him or her to a life of adventure and discovery.

· ·

**An interim's ability to navigate change
and feed off its energy leads him or her
to a life of adventure and discovery.**

· ·

Communication of Change

Whether orchestrating, leading, or delivering change, an interim is often engaged in communicating change. The communication of change, when strategically planned and delivered, effectively reinforces and enhances the leadership of change. An interim's experience of leading change in a wide range of organizations provides a deep well from which to draw when considering the psychology and implications of communication. For instance, organizations typically either under-communicate, in which case they fail to engage hearts and minds, or they over-communicate and confuse teams and leaders with unnecessary noise. There are few organizations in which the strategies, tone, and type of communication is perfect. For an interim leader navigating this to achieve "buy-in" of a proposed change is always a challenge.

What is the most important aspect of communicating change? To focus on the positive, the potential outcomes, rather than the disruptive impact. Change presents an opportunity, not a threat. An interim articulates the vision and results that a change offers and communicates this effectively to client leadership so that the change can be effectively promoted to key stakeholders. In these circumstances an interim is tuned into the organizational culture, although cautious not to assume too much, especially if the interim has worked on similar projects before. An interim understands the communication needs of all stakeholder groups and has expertise in planning the timing and most effective delivery method(s) for communication to stakeholders.

Clients often ask an interim leader to help create communications for senior leadership and other tiers of the workforce. This is largely because of the interim's experience and expertise. In addition to focusing on specific deliverables, an interim is tasked with communicating about those deliverables with slide decks and briefing papers. Rather than considering this out of scope, an interim sees these communications projects as effective tools for leveraging change. Communication is primarily the responsibility of internal leadership, but given the opportunity, an interim can enhance these communications by adding perspective, wisdom, clarity, and focus.

. . . .

An interim can enhance communications by adding perspective, wisdom, clarity, and focus.

. . . .

Embedding Change

Often an interim is responsible for moving the dial to deliver a change program within a short timeframe. An interim may not be with the organization long enough to fully see the change project's entire implementation. An interim may however be required to design processes to embed change over this longer period of time. In many ways this is more challenging for an interim than delivering the original change project under short time pressures. To create processes to successfully embed change an interim needs to calculate all the variables in the organization, processes, and people to create the best conditions for successful implementation—without having the opportunity to course-correct in real time.

. . . .

An effective interim has a commitment to the client to leave a legacy of significant value.

. . . .

When an interim leader completes the design of a change program and moves on, he or she often leaves a long-term impact or legacy. In fact, an effective interim has a commitment to the client to leave a legacy of significant value. As Robert Schaffer notes in *High Impact Consulting*, "Management consultants must be more than experts in their field. They must serve as effective change agents and share accountability with their clients for the ultimate outcome of their consulting projects." While this may appear to contradict the view held by Besondy and Travis that interims generally leave infrastructure to others, the emphasis on the "accountability for the ultimate outcome" includes planning for the long term. It is often necessary for an interim to work closely with the client's permanent leadership to plan implementation actions for the future; the need for these actions arises from the project that the interim has delivered. In this way, the change becomes embedded. The following example illustrates this:

EXAMPLE: Designing processes and tools for leaders

> An interim leader was engaged by a client to deliver a contract scope that included developing the senior leaders, organizational design, and coaching. The interim learned that the client's parent company was applying pressure for a slowdown of this work in order to reprioritize group strategy. The interim understood that the remaining term of his contract would not be sufficient to complete the coaching of senior managers begun months earlier. The interim spent the remaining six weeks of the contract designing processes that could be embedded in the organization over the long-term and provide leaders with tools to use on a day-to-day basis. For example, these included a mentoring program, line-manager coaching program, and a performance-management system upgrade. The interim discharged his responsibility to ensure that the changes he was able to implement would be adopted and continued by permanent leadership.

Often an interim will not see his or her projects implemented. This can be frustrating, or it can play into an interim's sweet-spot —moving on to a new change project in another organization. However, clients often rely on an interim to do more than work on a project and move on. When this occurs, the interim's contract can evolve into broader leadership in rolling out the change program. In these instances, the interim is embedded in the organization and stays long enough to see the effective implementation of the work he or she has led. Many interims find this to be tremendously rewarding; owning the outcomes of the design and recommendations in observing the impact on the organization.

The Confederation of British Industry discusses this in their business guide, *Interim Executive Management*: "Clients have found that interims are an effective strategic weapon to gain competitive advantage, through rapid and lasting change. They bring a refreshing degree of objectivity and prove excellent at building and leading internal teams and managing external suppliers – including consultants. Changes introduced in this way are far more resilient than those created and imposed by an outside agency." It is no surprise that an interim leader shows his or her effectiveness when designing, leading, and implementing change programs for clients.

CHAPTER 11

The Interim as Coach and Mentor

"Those who lead by example and demonstrate passion for what they do make it much easier for their followers to do the same."
— Marshall Goldsmith, *Harvard Business Review*

This chapter explores how an interim leader brings experience, wisdom, and insight to individuals within organizations as a coach or mentor. This "added value", is something that leaders should not underestimate. Executive coaching is an expensive development aid that delivers real results. Having an interim leader deliver a project, as well as coach senior leaders in their understanding of organizational development, often with a high degree of personal development, is a significant and valuable contribution!

A major component of what an interim leader brings to clients is an expertise as a coach and mentor. In fact, the likelihood that the interim will become a mentor or coach to leaders in the client organization is high. In their book *The Interim Manager,* Clutterbuck and Dearlove describe how some companies "explicitly state that part of the interim manager's brief should be to use his or her experience to 'mentor' more junior managers." Incumbent leaders realize quickly that they can tap into an interim's wealth of experience, wisdom, and insight. It is no accident that an experienced interim brings value to individual leaders as well as insight to an organization. In *Relational Coaching,* De Hann alludes to this:

> "Like a fragment of the hologram, the coachee presents a complete and personal image of the organization. Making use of this, the coach can often relate the coachee's problems and emotions to the problems and emotions prevailing within the coachee's organization."

. . . .

Incumbent leaders realize quickly that they can tap into an interim's wealth of experience, wisdom, and insight.

. . . .

An interim who has seen many organizations and worked alongside multiple leaders, often contributes to this diagnosis as he or she observes the organization's patterns and culture. Leaders often confide in an interim as an objective coach, who helps guide individuals, as well as organizations.

Many management thinkers draw a distinction between coaching and mentoring, but when it comes to the contribution of interim leaders there are blurred lines between these two disciplines. Interims offer professional and personal development and model best practices of leadership when engaged with client organizations. Interims serve other leaders by providing professional guidance in a coaching capacity, as well as engaging in a supportive master-apprentice mentoring relationship.

One of the key elements of coaching and mentoring is the ability to give feedback. Often an interim is called on for this, or occasions may arise when the interim may point out to a client when feedback is needed and the benefits of offering it.

Consider the following examples:

Example: Client leader solicits feedback

1. *An interim leader worked for a client for about a year and built strong relationships, including with the main sponsoring client. The client asked the interim if he was willing to provide feedback on the client's own effectiveness as a leader. The interim's response is a case study in giving feedback: "Let me give you feedback on what you do really well as a leader". Surprisingly, the client really wanted to hear the flip side of the coin, rather than any commendations. It is however advisable to point out the positives that someone offers before identifying areas for development. In the preceding weeks, the interim leader also received several comments from client employees that he could have included in his feedback to the client leader. When offering feedback, it is best to use first-hand examples and encapsulate other people's experiences within the same boundaries, i.e., avoid assumptions and "he/she thinks that you are ..." illustrations. The interim's overall experience of coaching this leader was a positive one and the relationship continued long after the specific interim engagement.*

Example: *Interim is "duty-bound" to offer candid feedback*

2. *The interim leader was working with a client on a significant project and had just delivered the first major milestone. The level of change was off the charts as the team focused on delivering this milestone. The key leader in the client organization had a style of working — highly creative, interventionist, and excitable — that drove some colleagues crazy. The interim leader felt a responsibility to offer feedback to this leader, if only for the sanity of the next phase of the project. The interim offered a conversation and was surprised when the client leader warmly and constructively received it. Sometimes client leaders are not defensive; they are grateful to have a respected professional offer insight.*

An interim is in a privileged position to give feedback. Interims see situations objectively and offer candid feedback without worries of organizational baggage, politics, and career suicide. In fact, client leaders and teams value and respect an interim's feedback as a coach and mentor, given the interim's experience and gravitas.

. . . .

Leaders and teams value and respect an interim's feedback as a coach and mentor, given the interim's experience and gravitas.

. . . .

The Interim as Coach

On a few occasions, an interim leader is hired specifically in the role of coach. For instance, this has happened once in the author's long career as an interim. The client, a government agency, hired the author to provide dedicated coaching to the Chief Human Resource Officer and the Management Development Manager. Neither of these leaders had much private sector experience, but they wanted to benefit from the interim's expertise while addressing specific projects in their domain. Although the assignment "ask" was not difficult, the follow-through was more challenging. Public sector and nonprofit sector organizations present different challenges with regards to levels of bureaucracy and timescales for implementing solutions. Of course, this is also affected by whether there are unions and what precisely is being addressed. In such a case, providing interim expertise as a coach involves bringing "best-practice" ideas to the table to guide leaders through the development and implementation phase of change projects. This is often a different experience than most interim roles, in which the interim is accountable to deliver a solution. It is, however, important for an interim to walk side-by-side with coachees to help them grow and deliver their agenda.

Often an interim's role as a coach to client leaders happens as a spin-off to their core assignment. For example, an interim leader's client offered the following when giving a reference: "His authenticity and integrity was an important supporting element in his effectiveness within and beyond the team. He is a very skilled and supportive coach and brings expertise resource to members of the team. He was continually sought out for support and input by many on a regular basis, including me." Such contributions are a regular occurrence for an interim.

An interim leader has experience in a wide range of organizations, cultures, and sectors, and brings deep insight. An interim has been immersed in leadership challenges and knows what works and what doesn't. It is essential that an interim offers feedback and input with humility, otherwise client leaders and teams will likely be less than receptive.

· ·

An interim leader has experience in a wide range of organizations, cultures, and sectors, and brings deep insight.

· ·

An interim's influence as a coach often stretches beyond the traditional definition of coaching. Some leadership development professionals paint a distinct difference between the role of a coach and a consultant; a coach helps the coachee find his or her own solutions to certain challenges, whereas a consultant is advisory and offers ideas, solutions, and options. An interim often finds him or herself in a hybrid role of doing both. An interim may coach a client to make significant professional changes and chart a voyage of self-discovery, as well as offering them advice, ideas, and solutions. An interim leader is a versatile, culturally-tuned coach with many tools in his or her bag.

While on client assignments, an interim can be asked questions about the rationale, intentions, and motivations of others. This can often arise as a result of others confiding in someone they believe to have an impartial and mature perspective. An interim offers insights, ideas, suggestions, and resolutions. Clients prize an interim leader's ability to coach both an organization as well as individuals. This role of a change coach is familiar territory for an interim and whether it is in service of coaching individuals or organizations, an interim demonstrates expertise as a confidant, fixer, trouble-shooter, and resolution-oriented professional.

• •

An interim demonstrates expertise as a confidant, fixer, trouble-shooter, and resolution-oriented professional.

• •

The best coaches have high emotional intelligence – a well-developed awareness of their personal, inter-personal, and con-textual emotional connection with those around them. What does an emotionally intelligent coach offer? In this case, an in-terim brings a high degree of self-awareness, and can quickly read others within the context of their environment. An interim's high-EQ coaching ability derives from a mixture of personality, experience, maturity, and sensitivity. An interim leader often de-velops his or her coaching prowess through time, but it has little to do with an interim's actual age. As Russell and Daniell point out in *Interim Management*: "Interim managers must of course be experienced but they must also have demonstrable track re-cord of success and achievement and that need not come with age." As an interim develops his or her craft during years of varying assignments, the interim is exposed to situations that further develop an interim's expertise as an emotionally intel-ligent coach.

The Interim as Mentor

A mentor is respected for his or her seniority, objectivity, and wisdom, especially in the master-apprentice model of mentor-ing. This is also the case for an interim leader. As well as gain-ing the expertise for which the interim was hired, the client organizations and leaders also get a senior business counsellor who adds value to the team. This is not always the case with consultants; the interim's role as mentor and coach is a primary difference between a consultant and an interim leader. An interim's contribution is rich in depth as well as breadth, and this comes from one individual. This depth and breadth is not as often evident with a consultant – at least when just invested in one person. When an interim offers mentoring to client leadership, the interim brings quality to his or her tenure, a contribution that exceeds the boundaries of the immediate project.

In *Everyone Needs a Mentor,* David Clutterbuck discusses the fact that mentors exercise four styles of behavior to help others learn – stretching, directive, non-directive, and nurturing. An interim rarely trains to be a professional mentor, but an interim's experience lends itself readily to this role and adds value to the client's experience. As a mentor, an interim embodies Clutterbuck's emphasis of the role's subtleties: "The core skill of a mentor can be described as having sufficient sensitivity to the mentee's needs to respond with the appropriate behaviors."

An interim leader typically offers mentoring support as an informal spin-off to their contribution, rather than as part of a formal assignment or mentoring program that may be offered in a client organization. The interim's relationship with senior leaders and executives often means that the interim can be a "listening ear" to these leaders. Clutterbuck discusses this aspect of executive mentoring and goes on to say, "To be effective, professional mentors have to have a broad knowledge and exposure to business direction, to the patterns of senior management thinking and behavior." An interim has often worked as a senior leader and with senior leaders while tackling significant organizational challenges; given this deep and varied experience an interim is an effective mentor.

Employees often latch onto an interim leader when they are looking for career advice. Employees develop a secure confidence in an interim, and perhaps see the interim as a "favorite uncle or aunt" who can be trusted to give impartial advice without breaking confidence. A careful balance needs to be struck here. An interim's role is objective but he or she needs to avoid becoming a listening post for discontents. Rather, an interim offers coaching and mentoring as support to those who genuinely want the interim's advice. An interim may for example, point a member of the client organization in the direction of further education options, networking groups, or conferences. An interim may also work with employees to help to define their ideal career paths. Whatever the opportunity, an interim can be an excellent foil for employees who are needing career guidance and suggestions for professional development.

There are many instances of an interim extending his or her core accountabilities by providing coaching and mentoring support for clients. This may be defined specifically as part of the interim project deliverables. However, clients may ask an interim to provide recommendations that are "off-piste". These can take the form of additional work streams or more informal conversations with senior leaders. For example, a CEO may ask an interim leader for feedback on the impact that members of the board are having on the organization. Depending on the challenges the CEO is facing with the board members, the interim's response may broaden into senior-level coaching and mentoring, giving advice on succession planning, culture building, and resourcing. As a versatile, experienced coach and mentor, particularly to senior leadership, an interim leader is of tremendous value in instances of broad organizational dynamics.

Kouzes and Posner discuss the virtue of "strengthening others" in *The Leadership Challenge*. Because an interim leader has such a rich and diverse career of doing just that, the interim's ability to coach and mentor others to strengthen those around him or her is of great value to client organizations, leadership, and teams.

CHAPTER 12

GREAT Interim Competencies

"It is not how much you do, but how much love you put into the doing that matters."

— Mother Teresa

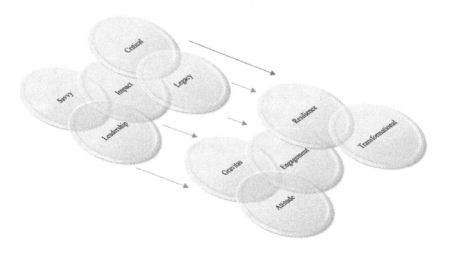

The SCILL Model© (*What*)   GREAT Competencies (*How*)

The SCILL Model© defines the DNA of an interim leader so clients can understand **what** an interim brings to the table—savvy, critical, impact, leadership, legacy. An interim leader is distinctive from other leaders not only by **what** an interim offers, but **how** he or she does it. Given that the SCILL Model© attributes are an interim's DNA, then the GREAT competencies are the enzymes that transcribe the DNA's code; for an interim, this translates into action – **how** an interim operates differentiates an interim from other leaders. The GREAT competencies offer clients a framework for understanding **how** an interim operates and assessing an interim leader's distinctive strengths.

The Confederation of British Industry describes an interim leader as, "proactive and results-oriented - having substantial change and transition leadership experience, a good communicator, and commanding attention and respect." This description in *Interim Executive Management* aligns well with the changing world of work; an interim leader has the competencies needed to deliver results in the workplace today –and in the future. William Bridges notes in *Job Shift* that success in the future world of work requires three critical characteristics: employability, vendor-mindedness, and resiliency. These characteristics are embodied in five essential interim leader competencies.

What are the critical competencies that an interim leader demonstrates?

- Gravitas
- Resilience
- Engagement
- Attitude (to excel)
- Transformational

Gravitas

When a leader makes an entrance or speaks, others quickly decide whether to take notice of him or her. A leader with gravitas –authority, weight, seriousness, and dignity —immediately commands respect and conveys importance. An interim, by virtue of his or her gravitas, is a recognized leader with a strong sense of responsibility and commitment.

An interim leader demonstrates gravitas by offering mature insight when facing a client's challenges; the interim draws on vast experience and expertise to earn the client's immediate respect. It is equally important that an interim leader display such gravitas on an ongoing, long-term basis. Gravitas demonstrates an interim leader's ability to understand, analyze, and interpret the dynamics of organizations and individuals. Ultimately, clients observe an interim leader's gravitas when the interim synthesizes solutions and makes powerful recommendations.

• •

An interim displays gravitas by synthesizing solutions and making powerful recommendations.

• •

Trustworthiness is another way in which an interim leader demonstrates gravitas. In fact, trustworthiness is fundamental to gravitas. If a client lacks trust in the interim's ability to deliver to the client's advantage, then the relationship will not succeed. Consider David Maister's discussion in *The Trusted Advisor* of "The Trust Equation":

$$T = \frac{C + R + I}{S}$$

T = trustworthiness, C = credibility, R = reliability, I = intimacy and S = self-orientation

An interim relates to the client in words, actions, emotions, and motives; these are each aligned to elements of The Trust Equation, described here in the context of interim leadership:

- **Trustworthiness** is based on the reputation an interim earns from previous assignments as well as his or her character developed as a leader through transition
- **Credibility** is established as a mark of an interim's expertise and ability to align to the client organization and project
- **Reliability** is proven through the interim's delivery
- **Intimacy** is demonstrated as the interim connects with leaders and colleagues, and is passionate about the value he or she brings
- **Self-orientation** is evident through the interim's focus on delivering for the client with an expendability; the interim embraces the temporary nature of his or her tenure

An interim leader's expertise and ability to deliver results reinforces an interim's gravitas. In addition to such professional expertise, gravitas is also on display through the many elements of an interim leader's personal brand – how one is perceived. This brand is of course accentuated by a leader's appearance, vocabulary, and presence. Typically, an interim leader is a C-suite professional and dresses the part in a business suit unless the client's dress code is business casual. An interim speaks with respect and decorum, shows professionalism when discussing other client examples, and in every way exudes the poise and confidence one expects of a leader with gravitas.

Gravitas is charismatic and compelling. Clients seek an interim leader who demonstrates gravitas and are attracted by an interim's strength and success, especially when it is consistent. There is nothing as harmful to an interim's reputation than when a client tests an interim's understanding of an issue, only to be confronted with flimsy opinions, frivolous comments, or tepid attempts at solutions. Given an interim's experience with diverse clients across sectors and possibly across geographic regions, an interim exudes confidence and offers engaging perspectives. This may include a glimpse into the interim's wide-ranging interests, hobbies, and accomplishments. Such stories and perspectives reveal the interim to be a capable and fascinating colleague; this often spurs a potential client to engage the interim for an assignment.

· ·

An interim exudes confidence and offers engaging perspectives.

· ·

Resilience

Building a successful interim career requires resilience. An interim leader promotes him or herself in the marketplace based on the interim's potential to add value, his or her track-record, and self-belief. An interim needs the "vendor-mindedness" described by Bridges, a consciousness that he or she is a commodity with a value that is greater than the cost to the client.

A leader who is used to organizational stability or who lacks the tenacity to develop a network and seek assignments, will not succeed as an interim. When an assignment finishes, this can be an uncertain time for an interim leader. This shift does however provide an interim an opportunity for business development, networking, and reflection. Clearly, an interim needs a degree of financial stability to get the best out of these times. An interim builds a financial cushion to ride out periods between assignments. That said, an interim is also more comfortable with the risk associated with gaps between assignments than the average leader. Being comfortable with risk is one of the reasons an interim shows resilience in the face of change.

An interim is more comfortable with risk than the average leader.

When being considered for new assignments, an interim, like any professional, is not guaranteed success. There are times when a client may reject an interim. The secret to success for an interim is to be resilient, to learn from each experience and bounce back strongly. Sometimes the project is not the right one, or the client-interim chemistry isn't the right fit, or there is competition and someone else is more appropriate for the assignment. An interim leader's resilient character enables an interim to develop his or her career based on a portfolio of successful projects, multiple relationships, and a tenacity to make a difference.

Engagement

What does full engagement mean? An interim leader engages in a client project for more than a paycheck. An interim engages with a client in a fully invested way; this is essential to bring maximum value. There is a big difference between leaders who show up to express their expertise and those who care about the organization and its people as though their reputation is made or broken by the professional engagement. In many ways, an interim is well-suited to the "culture of consent", described by Charles Handy in *The Age of Unreason,* a culture in which "intelligent people prefer to agree rather than to obey." In other words, an interim chooses to commit professionally, emotionally, and with a passion, not just to do a job

An interim often regards a client as his or her "company." An interim leader cares about the client's success, builds strong relationships, and is fully vested in the outcome of the project.

As Robert Schaffer states in *High-Impact Consulting*:

> "Only consultants who share a strong sense of responsibility for client successes or failures and who treat each consulting project as a valuable personal learning experience for themselves and their clients can hope to become effective partners with those clients."

Often, clients regard an interim as a temporary leader who is absorbed into the organization, rather than a temporary resource who is assisting the organization. This makes a big difference. In fact, leaders in client organizations are often shocked to discover that an interim is not a permanent employee. When fully engaged, the interim's professional, commercial, and emotional bond with a client is almost seamless.

. . . .

Leaders in client organizations are often shocked to discover that an interim is not a permanent employee.

. . . .

It is essential for an interim leader on assignment to be an engaged and curious member of the team, as well as being a team player who has a will to connect and a mind to learn. As Alasdair Drysdale suggests in *The Interim Director*, "One of the best ways to get people onside with you rapidly is to ask their advice. The fact that you consider someone to be knowledgeable and sensible enough to give such advice is a subliminal statement that you respect their judgement."

It is equally critical that an interim demonstrates his or her committed engagement by a resolve to make things happen. As Richard Lindenmuth notes in *The Outside the Box Executive*, "If you are determined to make a project successful, and you provide resources and support to the individuals and teams responsible for the success, their resolve and determination will be reinforced." This commitment to colleagues is essential for an interim who seeks credibility for his or her contribution.

Parting company with a client offers an insight to the level of engagement between the interim and client. An interim invests significant energy in the client's leaders who he or she may have coached, and with whom the interim has built deep relationships while working through major projects. When a contract closes, an interim often feels a degree of, "I can still do so much more." But the pragmatic choice of the interim journey is to balance the temptation of prolonging engagements with the pursuit of new assignments. Each assignment is an opportunity for an interim to engage fully with leaders, teams, projects, and organizations; essential to bring out the best in an interim's contribution.

Attitude (to excel)

This may appear as an obvious competency, but an interim cannot underestimate the importance of having an attitude of winning, challenging, and exceeding expectations. In *Built To Last,* Collins and Porras paint a picture of highly visionary companies as "having self-confidence bordering on hubris." Much like these visionary companies, an interim with hubris, pride, confidence, and professional excellence can deliver outstanding results. An interim needs to also balances hubris with humility.

An interim brings a winning "attitude" to client engagements. An interim is not just joining an organization, playing a role, or working to live. An interim challenges the status quo, provokes visionary thinking, makes waves, punctures patterns, and raises the flag of achievement.

• •

An interim challenges the status quo, provokes visionary thinking, makes waves, punctures patterns, and raises the flag of achievement.

• •

An interim expects to be confronted with challenging, unexpected paradigms with which he or she does not agree. An interim also expects to discover paradigms that are inspiring and thought-provoking. Whether these paradigms exist in the same client organization is less important than how an interim addresses them. As presented in detail in the SCILL Model© discussion, an interim's relational savvy expertise is essential in such situations. An interim offers critical commentary and challenges existing paradigms while also offering alternative solutions. This leads to successful relationships and results. When demonstrating a positive attitude towards the client for example, an interim explains various scenarios, unpacks cause and effect, and pro-vides leading-edge research to challenge assumptions.

When striving to deliver with an attitude to excel, it is vital that an interim, within the context of a client relationship, balances his or her challenge to the status quo with an attitude of respect. Having an attitude is often interpreted as having an "edge". This mindset to excel, offer an alternative perspective, see through a different lens, and raise one's voice when others acquiesce, is how an interim contributes a constructive, creative, and chal-lenging attitude.

Transformational

The most frequent context in which an interim thrives is lead-ing change, as discussed in Chapter 10. It is part of an interim's DNA to have a healthy discontentment with the status quo. An interim not only seeks opportunities to lead change, he or she possesses a fundamental competency of being transformational. One of the client testimonials in Chapter 2 describes an interim as a "change junkie". An interim projects possibilities, specu-lates synergies, devises designs, and injects impetus. An interim leader is a disruptive, yet productive, influence. Clients engage an interim leader to lead major transformation, move blockag-es, fast-track projects, and achieve big goals. An interim's appe-tite to make a difference is huge. This is one of the main reasons an interim chooses this career.

Clients engage an interim leader to lead major transformation, move blockages, fast-track projects, and achieve big goals.

Without champions and masters of change, organizations do not move forward. This is why an interim leader is so valuable. In *The End of Jobs,* Taylor Pearson states, "It's the work of understanding and operating in the complex and chaotic systems – entrepreneurship, that's increasingly in demand." This is home-base for an interim leader who is focused on transformational rather than incremental organizational change.

For many organizations, an interim's ability to lead change is a tremendous boost. Such transformation needs to occur in a concentrated period of time and in specific applications. As discussed in Chapter 10, accelerated change needs to be matched with periods of integration, application, and consolidation. Transformative influence is essential to future-proof organizational growth. As Robert Schaffer notes in *High-Impact Consulting,* "The ability to make things happen, to effect change, is the most critical dimension of organizational success."

An interim leader's connection with transformation may sound dramatic – an interim burns energy fast and replenishes through a "high-carb" diet of new challenges —but an interim leader is a distinctive resource that serves an essential need. An interim is a highly skilled change catalyst, motivated to deliver successful outcomes.

PART IV

Engaging Interim Leaders

CHAPTER 13

Hiring Interims

Part IV of the book focuses on various aspects of engaging an interim leader for an assignment; this includes the life cycle of engagement from the perspective of both the client and interim, which is important given the partnership involved. For a client, hiring an interim is a significant investment in a high-value resource. For an interim, being hired by a client is a privilege and a responsibility to deliver on the client's expectations.

For clients who have not hired an interim before, the first time can be an eye-opener. For some clients it is like planting a spring bulb, expecting one flower to appear and being surprised when multiple flowers bloom from that one bulb. An interim is not just a one-trick pony with a narrow skill set. An interim leader has a skill set that is incredibly well developed and intensely valuable for organizations and brings a treasure trove of other gifts as well.

. . . .

An interim has a skill set that is incredibly well developed and intensely valuable for organizations.

. . . .

What does the client need to know about hiring an interim leader? This chapter explores the essentials that a client needs to consider when hiring the right interim for a project:

- Timeframe
- Finding an Interim
- Multiple Clients
- Relationships

Timeframe

Most interim contracts are full-time engagements with a client, although some might morph into part-time depending on the needs of the client. An interim does not frequently dip in and out of multiple clients simultaneously since the interim is a dedicated resource. For many clients, hiring an interim can take significant risk out of the immediate need for a critical resource. This is often not to fill a permanent headcount on a temporary basis, rather sourcing a specific skill-set to deliver organizational change and/or projects. Permanent leadership appointments may well follow or change, and an interim's tenure is sometimes a contributing factor in subsequent appointment decisions.

As Taylor Pearson notes in *The End of Jobs*, "Instead of a large, up-front investment in hiring and training someone who may or may not be good enough for the role, you're able to make a small investment, over time, in someone who has been vetted by other people in your industry." This small investment is relative of course to the long-term and full employment costs of a permanent resource. Investing in an interim does allow the client to advance their agenda and make permanent resourcing decisions over a longer period.

An interim often has a time limit in working for the same client. There are various reasons for this:

- An interim expands his or her experience by having diverse clients, which makes him or her more valuable to future clients.
- An interim's impact tends to diminish the longer the tenure with the same client. While this may vary for each interim, the greatest shift an interim can make in organizational development is within the first six months of a contract.
- The longer the contract, the greater the chance that the interim may "go native" and become part of the day-to-day organizational apparatus.
- Being expendable and leaving a legacy is a sign of success.
- An interim needs new challenges.

Clients need to understand the rationale for an interim working in multiple and diverse organizations to appreciate the value an interim brings. This diversity differentiates the interim's contribution from other resource options. An interim has worked from the inside-out for many organizations, unlike consultants, who often work from the outside-in. An interim also has a perspective that is noticeably richer than candidates on the job market. These are critical reasons why an interim leader brings unique value.

. . . .

An interim has worked from the inside-out for many organizations, unlike consultants, who often work from the outside-in.

. . . .

Finding Interims

Clients seeking an interim leader often refer to interim agencies. There are many of these, but they are not all the same. Some retain true interim professionals on their books, and others use the term "interim" loosely to describe professionals who are temporary contractors. Some interim agencies focus on professional entrepreneurs, others on retired executives, and others are broader in their range of clients and interims. Resources on Interim Agencies at the end of this book provide some contact details. Otherwise, a client's Internet search will provide a wealth of contacts.

Apart from making client connections through interim agencies, many interims develop relationships with clients through networking. There are some who would argue that networking is the best method for connecting with clients. There is, however, real value in agencies that make introductions to clients for the best interims, having vetted them and matched them with the specific client need.

To ensure a successful choice of the right interim, the client needs to look beyond the interim's CV for evidence of delivery. The client can expect the interim to be excited about his or her achievements as well as the client's challenges, and should listen for effective collaboration and leadership, as well as vetting references. The client needs to also weigh the intangibles: Is the interim a savvy leader? Is he or she sharp, insightful, creative, humorous, thoughtful, intelligent, expertly and culturally tuned-in? An interview can determine whether an interim is the right fit for their project and organization by using the guidelines found throughout this book, particularly the GREAT competencies in Chapter 12, and the SCILL Model© Assessment for sourcing interims in Chapter 16.

Choosing carefully is important. A client should be immediately impressed by an interim, and once engaged, by their results that deliver value. There are many factors for clients to consider. As mentioned previously, an effective interim chooses to develop a diverse portfolio of projects and clients; this is a strength. There are some exceptions. A new interim may enter the market with considerable experience in the corporate or consulting world, but not be seasoned as an interim leader. When an interim has a long CV of interim assignments it does not necessarily mean that he or she is right for the client. Some interims have majored in specific industry sectors and like to stay on familiar ground. Others have worked for a certain type of client, such as the public sector, and are not well-suited to cultures in other types of client organizations. Some interims have a strong desire to make an impact; others are on a road to retirement and enjoy short-term projects in which they impart wisdom and then move on.

For many leaders, the challenge of hiring a temporary seasoned expert to expedite a surge of change within an organization is an unfamiliar concept. The primary options are to reach out to a consultancy or to recruit a permanent leader. An interim leader is a sound strategic and commercial alternative. What are some of the questions clients have about hiring an interim? Beyond the basic question "What is an interim?" clients want to know the cost and value. The cost of engaging an interim is often lower than engaging a consultancy, and the opportunity cost is not to be minimized. The cost of an interim leader is also likely to be less than the full employment costs of a permanent leader, given that no benefits or organizational overheads are incurred.

Setting the bar high with measurable outcomes that carry significant value to the organization is precisely the playing field of an interim leader. An interim expects to be asked to deliver big goals and welcomes it when clients tap their considerable expertise and experience.

. . . .

An interim expects to be asked to deliver big goals.

. . . .

Multiple Clients

The calling card of a credible interim is a significant project delivered for a client. A diversity of clients and projects also gives an interim a broad range of skills. Whether an interim's portfolio goes deep and narrow or deep and broad, the common factor is "deep" –an interim is an expert. As an interim develops his or her career, the interim takes pride in a growing list of clients and successful outcomes. Multiple clients build the gravitas expected of an interim; an interim is shaped by diverse experiences, major achievements, and many relationships.

McGovern and Russell state in *A New Brand of Expertise*, "Demand for intellectual capital may be high, but the independent consultant must contend with the relative obscurity he or she will inherit when no longer bound to a traditional corporate patrimony." This is unlikely to deter an interim as the transition from employment to freelance carries with it an opportunity to build a brand, reputation, and track-record of success. An interim's successful projects and clients provide a tapestry of references.

· ·

An interim's successful projects and clients provide a tapestry of references.

· ·

Some of the best interim leaders have found that beginning an interim career is the greatest challenge. A client who is prepared to offer a contract to an interim leader when the interim does not have other successful interim contracts on his or her CV must be sure that the interim is the right fit for the project. In these cases, a client can select an interim based on the merits of the individual leader and the closest match of his or her expertise to the project in question. Clients can use the SCILL Model© and the GREAT competencies as a framework for assessment. The client may be the first in an eventual list of multiple clients of a highly successful interim leader!

An interim chooses to engage in a portfolio career to move the dial in many organizations and contribute successfully wherever he or she has an opportunity. As William Bridges states in *Job Shift*, "Sometimes the composite career is a way to express those parts of oneself that are excluded from the narrow world of the job ... it provides the chance to do a number of different things and thereby gain the security of diversification and the personal rewards of variety." As an interim gains experience and grows his or her list of clients and projects, the interim can eloquently discuss previous assignments as evidence of his or her expertise for future clients.

Relationships

Relationships are vital for an interim. An effective interim has significant relationships with agencies and professionals in the industry, previous clients, networking contacts, and probably some professional media outlets. As Dembitz and Essinger state in *Breakthrough Consulting*, "working relationships with your clients are the most valuable asset you possess."

How can clients seeking to hire an interim predict an interim's ability to build successful relationships? Why is this important to the success of the interim engagement? Clients need to consider these aspects:

- Relationship savvy
- Trusted advisor
- Elements of successful client relationships
- Communication style
- Bulletproof relationships
- Solid references
- Evidence of strong networks

An interim's relationship savvy yields tangible benefits that extend well beyond the scope of the project. For example, he or she is likely to have a rich network of professional contacts who may prove helpful in new assignments. Clients benefit because the interim is stimulating and brings gravitas in a way that enhances the caliber of leadership and team collaboration. An interim has a different pace in the way he or she works, brings a different perspective to the organization, and builds relationships in a manner that exudes confidence. Clients find that an interim is bold in the management of relationships, in that he or she is prepared to challenge accepted paradigms and the status quo. An interim is also intent on building trust and collaboration in the consideration of change. An interim is a professional of interest and often proves to be a rich source of value in client and team relationships.

An interim is bold in the management of relationships, in that he or she is prepared to challenge accepted paradigms and the status quo.

An interim's ability to build relationships within client organizations is critical to the success of interim assignments. What is an interim's communication style? Walking the corridors, connecting with teams and individuals, picking up the phone and speaking with people, and attending stakeholder meetings, are all legitimate ways that an interim builds an important reservoir of relationships.

Relationships between a client and an interim have many critical elements:

- **Mutual respect**

  Clients engage an interim because they need an expert to deliver results. An interim's track record and professional stature means that the interim-client relationship is likely to have a high degree of respect. A client should also test that the interim has mutual respect of the client organization, the assignment challenge, and the leaders with whom the interim will engage. An interim's achievements, personality, demeanor, and attitude all contribute to a good fit for the client.

- **Shared vision and goals**

  One of Stephen Covey's seven habits of highly effective people is, "seek first to understand and then to be understood." Clients often appreciate an interim leader's objective input and insight on their vision and goals. Clients should be wary of an interim who jumps to conclusions, rolls out a solution that worked for another client, or demonstrates arrogance about understanding the client context. Reaching consensus of the vision and goals of the assignment are an early prerequisite in establishing a strong working relationship with an interim.

- **Invested value**

    If a client believes that the relationship with an interim is bringing demonstrable value, they will be more likely to invest in that relationship. If an interim receives feedback from the client that he or she is delivering excellent results and showing great leadership, the interim is likely to invest increased time and energy with the client to ensure success.

When does a client consider an interim to be a trusted advisor? This occurs when confidence and inspiration are partnered with collaboration and humility. A client's relationship with an interim is often experienced within the context of periods of change and transition, and typically results in a bond between leaders that lasts for many years.

A client often experiences that an interim is not a "Yes" person. He or she is prepared to challenge and contradict, as well as coerce and collaborate. An interim's role is not to be "liked", but to be "trusted". However, an effective interim knows how to build trust as well as be liked, all within the context of being a catalyst for change. A client often experiences an interim as an objective expert as well as an invested leader and collaborator.

· ·

An interim will challenge and contradict, as well as coerce and collaborate.

· ·

Occasionally, a client-interim relationship hits turbulence. In fact, if this isn't the case, an interim may not be carrying out his or her role effectively. An interim questions and challenges, and this sometimes results in the client dealing with periods of turbulence as the interim tests the assignment's boundaries and the need for organizational change. These "project-based" challenges are to be expected. An interim may also step on relational toes as part of his or her contribution. For example, this might occur in the context of organizational design or when analyzing the capability mix of existing leadership teams. Whatever the circumstances, an interim needs to develop an approachability and an authenticity to establish the best relationships and strive to ensure positive outcomes for the client. Often an interim's intervention benefits the client with a sharper strategy and clear path forwards.

CHAPTER 14

The Contract

Once a client decides to search for a suitable interim leader, there are numerous contractual considerations that need to be thought through. These include scope, confidentiality, and compensation, as well as aspects that are specific to an interim leader as compared with employees, consultants, and other resource options.

Consider this description of an interim leader from the *New York Times*, as quoted in The Confederation of British Industry's business guide, *Interim Executive Management*:

> "Interims go into a company for a short period to fix problems on a daily rate, without all the bells and whistles that accompany so many pay packages. In essence, they like to make changes and move on, rather than manage a stable situation or jockey for position in the hierarchy of a large corporation."

An interim's "contract mindset" is shaped by his or her drive to take on short-term, high-energy assignments that demand a sophisticated level of expertise. What factors should a client who is ready to hire an interim consider when developing the assignment contract?

- Psychological
- Internal or External?
- Term
- Finances

Psychological

An interim has a strong connection with the work that he or she does as well as the client's organization. In *The Gig Economy* Diane Mulcahy cites a 2015 study conducted by the Freelancers Union and Upwork:

> ". . .independent workers indicate that they are more satisfied with their work, and more engaged. They value autonomy, flexibility, and greater control they have by not being a full-time employee, and in many cases, they earn more."

Psychologically, this is why an interim is likely to make a positive contribution to the client's organization. It is critical that clients consider the psychological relationship that will exist once they hire an interim leader.

Client's Perspective

The client needs to appreciate that an interim is an expert who is motivated to deliver results and make a difference. An interim is not seeking a trial period before the offer of a permanent position and does not expect to ease his or her way into a team and project. An interim will hit the ground running. To be ready, the client needs to have lined up the required support structure, such as security access, laptop, introductory meetings, clear brief, and notification of colleagues. Most importantly, the client needs to dedicate time up front to the interim, point him or her in the desired direction, agree on methods of planning, communication, and documentation, and have clearly defined deliverables and timelines. The client should expect the interim to move quickly, ask questions, knock on doors, and generally dig into everything connected with the project. An interim will make waves, push the organization, look for quick response times, and challenge the status quo. The client needs to consider this when hiring an interim and be prepared.

· ·

An interim will move quickly, ask questions, knock on doors, and generally dig into everything connected with the project.

· ·

Interim Leader's Perspective

An effective interim understands that the client will not be one-hundred-percent dedicated to the project—the client hired the interim to fill this gap and show leadership. A successful interim anticipates the client's needs and identifies the most efficient way of getting information, reporting progress, and getting reviews of the project deliverables. An interim leader needs to be clear about the client's expectations and offer suggestions to the client as to how the interim will work. As discussed in depth in the SCILL Model© section, an interim needs to be savvy, and understand the organization's politics and culture, including the protocols of hierarchy. If an interim is working virtually, he or she needs to be clear about preferred methods of contact. For example, a client may prefer phone conversations to emails; the interim works out when this is most efficient and timely. As part of the psychological contract, an interim also needs to build relationships and a reputation of leadership and gravitas. This ensures that client leadership and their teams see the interim as more than just an "outsider" who delivers specific objectives.

Internal or External?

An effective interim leader can become so engaged with a client organization that its senior stakeholders forget that the interim is only committed to a contractual term. For the client, extending an interim contract can be an essential, positive decision. However, if the client retains an interim for continuity there can be risks. The longer an interim remains with a client, there is an increased likelihood that leadership and teams will view the interim as an internal resource. While this can be positive for the purposes of integration and collaboration, there are significant red flags. For example, this can signify that an organization has over-absorbed an interim, instead of addressing a permanent resourcing strategy. An interim's ability to be proactive with his or her exit strategy ensures that the interim remains objective, relevant, and sharp. By developing an exit strategy, an interim also helps the client consider long-term organizational design needs.

A successful interim joins a client organization with the intention of integrating with existing leadership rather than remaining aloof. Yes, an interim is a hired specialist resource, but he or she needs to fuse with the client organization to gain traction and support for his or her deliverables. A seasoned interim knows how to build effective relationships. In fact, an interim knows these are critical to delivering results. On a broader topic, the client needs to agree with the interim concerning internal activities in which he or she is expected to engage. For example, it may be useful for an interim to participate in culture workshops to understand the client's organization, but not to attend town-hall meetings. This might seem obvious, but the client and interim need to establish expectations early on and clarify any assumption in conversation and in writing.

. . . .

An interim needs to fuse with the client organization to gain traction and support for deliverables.

. . . .

Term

Typically, a client will propose a three-month initial term for a new interim contract. The client needs to see a return on value and contain any risk exposure. An interim leader invariably has confidence in his or her ability to add to or exceed the value-add to the client and rarely has an issue with the contract duration. It is important, however, that an interim be realistic and not over- or under-value his or her contribution. An interim leader is confident, has a track record of success, and a strong belief in the value he or she brings; an interim often impresses a client by delivering results—while showing gravitas, and how genuine, credible, and vital a leader he or she is. For many clients, an interim leader's availability is crucial. For that reason, it is important for an interim to market his or her services effectively and be ready on short notice for a new client contract.

An interim contract usually begins as a full-time commitment; it sometimes shifts to a part-time arrangement once the interim has broken the back of the assignment or as a response to fluctuations in organizational development. Not only is this pragmatic for the client, it allows an interim the flexibility to work for other clients as well as dig into business, professional, and personal development.

Other contract considerations involve time off. The client and interim need to discuss this in detail when the contract is negotiated. Typically, an interim may begin a contract with a client, having already communicated that a vacation is planned, or a short-term commitment with a previous client falls within the contract term. Being up-front about this shows an interim's professionalism. Often a client is happy for an interim to simply not work certain dates or make up the time. If possible, it is most beneficial for planning purposes if an interim leader schedules any vacation at the end of a client contract. Also, for tax purposes, this helps create a clean break in the contractual relationship should there be an audit of the client-interim relationship.

A break between client contracts is an opportunity, not a fearful prospect for an interim. A seasoned, successful interim finishes a client contract with a "check" in the boxes of achievements – and with strong relationships. The end of a client contract provides an opportunity for an interim to invest in future contracts. This includes the self-development and networking that are the mark of a successful interim. In fact, in between contracts an interim often over-indulges in networking and business development.

As Diane Mulcahy notes in *The Gig Economy*, "a broad network is important because it introduces the benefits of *weak ties* into our lives. It turns out that weak ties are the key to new opportunities." A savvy interim masters the art of developing "weak ties". As an interim networks in search of his or her next opportunity, the interim also catches up on reading, professional certification, developing a digital footprint, and other productive forms of self-development and marketing.

Finances

Compensation for interims takes into consideration the fact that an interim is a contractor and does not receive the employee benefits provided to permanent employees. This is one reason an interim's daily rate needs to be commensurate with their expertise and status. An interim has chosen to trade a steady income and benefits package for the higher monetary compensation offered for contract assignments and the enhanced flexibility that an interim career offers. For an interim, providing for pension, healthcare, and unpaid vacation is a price worth paying in return for the challenges and rewards of an interim career.

Most clients are willing to compensate an interim for the high value he or she adds. While an interim's rate may seem expensive, clients who consider the interim's expertise, short tenure, track record of success, along with the lack of other employee costs, understand the compelling business case for hiring an interim. An interim is a premium resource hired to deliver premium projects for a premium outcome and enhanced client value.

. . . .

An interim is a premium resource hired to deliver premium projects for a premium outcome and enhanced client value.

. . . .

Client needs vary; some clients prefer a daily rate and others an hourly rate. Some are cautious and negotiate a short contract and others jump in with a long-term duration. If a client is working through an agency, then the contract is between this intermediary and the client; the interim also negotiates with the agency rather than the client. The agency negotiates on behalf of the client and the interim to reach an agreeable contract. If a client negotiates a contract directly with the interim, the parties needs to ensure that the contract is legal and mutually acceptable.

Interim agencies provide valuable connections between clients and interims, and conduct important work developing client opportunities, vetting interims, and making client-interim connections. An agency takes a commission on the interim's rate. An agency depends on the interim to deliver excellent work to a client; this ensures that the agency receives an on-going commission. An agency proactively works with an interim as well as the client during the contract to ensure that all parties are delivering on expectations. Sources for locating interim agencies are included at the end of this book.

An offer of an extended contract is typically an opportunity for further negotiation; here are three typical scenarios:

1. The interim's value to the client has usually increased, given the traction the interim has gained and the reputation he or she has hopefully earned.
2. The client can reflect on the value of an interim and make adjustments to what the client considered a risk when agreeing to the initial terms; the client might also wish to offer a longer contract to secure the interim's services.

3. The agency reaps the benefits of a longer than expected contract and related commissions; the agency may consider rewarding the interim by taking a lower commission from the contracted rate.

When negotiating interim contracts clients should focus on the interim's value rather than cost. Often, the risk of not hiring an interim and benefitting from his or her expertise to accelerate change and deliver results, is immeasurably higher than the cost of hiring an interim.

CHAPTER 15

Interim Integration

For the client, the integration of an interim leader is a more complex and subtle exercise than onboarding a consultant or permanent employee. To be effective, an interim is integrated with permanent leadership, but not so glued in that he or she has an air of permanence. Typically, a client will include an interim on the team, yet encourage him or her to be objective, even disruptive, in the spirit of leading change.

David Maister notes in *The Trusted Advisor*, "None of us begins our career as a trusted advisor, but that is the status to which most of us aspire." Clearly, an interim leader hopes to be a trusted advisor to assist the client's organization with its growth aspirations. An interim reaches the position of trusted advisor relatively quickly due to his or her expertise, maturity, and gravitas. The relationship of an interim with the client is based on trust and yet has moments of tension as the interim spins a web of challenge, inspiration, and transformation.

How does an interim leader integrate into the client's organization, culture, team, and manage projects? It is important for both an interim and the client to understand these dynamics to build a successful relationship. The client makes the decision to hire an interim leader to inject expertise and objectivity into the organization; the interim delivers the results the client expects. To ensure a strong working relationship, it is essential that the interim and client consider these aspects of interim integration:

- Organization
- Culture
- Teams
- Projects

Organization

Often a client hires an interim leader to fulfil a role that is regarded as a more of a permanent than temporary position. The interim is engaged for a specific time in the organization's lifecycle to deliver a specific impact. For an interim, integrating into an organization isn't just about delivering results, it's about aligning with the organization's purpose and goals. As Dembitz and Essinger state in *Breakthrough Consulting*, "Working hard is insufficient if you are not also effective, and you can only be truly effective if you have a sincere empathy for your client's aims."

For an interim, integrating into an organization isn't just about delivering results, it's about aligning with the organization's purpose and goals.

It is highly likely that the client will include an interim leader in the organization's leadership team rather than use the interim for occasional external input. This creates a healthy environment in a number of ways:

1. An interim brings an immediate "voice of significance" to the leadership.

   Typically an interim has held C-Suite or senior leadership roles as well as other key interim roles in many organizations. An interim brings a significant presence to any leadership team. A client organization that recognizes the interim leader's value will take advantage of it rather than seeking immediate permanent recruitment or consultancies. It's like bringing a seasoned veteran onto a sport team's coaching staff to add broader perspective, mentor inexperienced team members, and elevate perspectives. Because of his or her track record, an interim commands immediate respect. When an interim speaks and leads, he or she demonstrates gravitas, maturity, and insight.

2. An interim challenges existing levels of leadership.

   Client leaders expect an interim to bring an edge to the existing team. Some client leaders may in fact be intimidated by an interim. An interim raises the bar of contribution, and usually comes with a stellar CV and diverse experiences. Leadership and teams feel an interim's impact on the organization immediately. This can be a great motivator for other leaders to raise their game and look to an interim as a role model.

3. An interim injects fresh ideas, direction, and energy.

   It is inevitable that an interim will bring fresh ideas and contributions. The interim may gush with activity that can at times be overwhelming. An interim is driven to achieve successful outcomes. An interim is quick to process information and challenges, and profuse in his or her production of organizational change activity.

For an interim, being in a leadership role offers a challenge that fuels the interim's engines of influence and impact. Clients often ask an interim to engage in projects beyond the scope of the current assignment. Clients appreciate that an interim brings wide experience to organizational challenges, assimilates requirements and solutions quickly, and gets results with few side-show issues. An interim rarely has an issue with scope-creep and enjoys being versatile and adaptable. An interim is focused on getting results rather than any political nuances, the next performance appraisal, or being considered in a succession plan.

As discussed earlier, an interim is like a seasoned veteran who joins the coaching staff of a sports team. Owners of sports teams will sometimes bring in a rescue specialist after the team's manager is fired following a run of poor results. For example, in the UK Premiership Football (Soccer) League, teams panic when they are deep in the season and performance on the field is not up to par. Team owners often fire the manager to avoid the financial impact of being relegated to a lower league. At this juncture, a list of rescue specialists are candidates to be the next manager. These rescue specialists revise playing strategies, motivate players, and bring a renewed sense of the optimism to clubs. This is much like the impact of an interim leader.

An interim creates strategy, anticipates the future, and steers change so that the organization is able to meet challenges. An interim shifts direction to avoid failure and breathes new life into tired colleagues. An interim's energy, optimism, and confidence are intoxicating. An interim can make the difference between a turgid journey or a disappointing outcome, and a renewed purpose for a team that is ready to achieve exciting goals.

. . . .

An interim creates strategy, anticipates the future, and steers change so that the organization is able to meet challenges.

. . . .

The integration of an interim into an organization, even as a "rescue specialist", is temporary. An interim's ability to integrate, detach, and integrate quickly into the next culture is part of this professional's agility. Sometimes an interim feels a sense of loss and disappointment when leaving a client. This demonstrates the degree of integration achieved. However, interims view client engagements as time-bound; this ensure that the interim remains effective.

Interestingly, in *Job Shift* William Bridges discusses a world with less permanency of jobs: "It destroys a sense of community that existed in many workplaces, and so it can be very lonely." While understanding Bridges' warning, most interims choose to look at the upside of an interim career; it exposes them to many communities and enables them to build relationships that they wouldn't otherwise have had the opportunity to enjoy. At the same time, some interims demonstrate characteristics of mavericks or loners –something for organizations to be aware of when selecting and assimilating them.

Culture

Integrating into the client's organizational culture is an important consideration for both the interim and the client. On the one hand, it is important for an interim to integrate so he or she understands and appreciates the organization. It is also important for an interim to remain one step removed from the culture to avoid being influenced by group-think or homogeneous opinions. In many ways, an interim is like a chameleon. An interim leader needs to adapt to client surroundings without losing the skills that make an interim effective.

Many interim assignments offer the opportunity to impact culture. In many ways, it is easier to do this from the inside, than it is to overlay something from the outside. This is different from a consultancy delivering culture change workshops; when internal leaders promote change, an interim has the opportunity to be part of the change inspired from within the organization. Indeed, an interim is a highly effective culture change agent, bringing illustrations and ideas that inspire others.

· ·
An interim is a highly effective culture change agent, bringing illustrations and ideas that inspire others.
· ·

An effective interim avoids trying to influence culture change without integration. This includes, for example, refraining from over-referencing previous organizations and clients. The author has had experiences with leaders who take on a key role in a new organization and during their first few months of employment, constantly reference his or her previous organizations. An interim leader is careful not to refer to previous clients as carbon copies when recommending change. Integration means taking on the character and challenges of the client organization and grappling with them shoulder-to-shoulder with client leaders and teams.

Culture is often illustrated by the stories that colleagues share. Whenever an interim integrates into a new organization, he or she will bring stories! An interim has experiences with diverse clients across many sectors and geographies. An interim has interacted with a wide spectrum of professionals and delivered projects through times of significant organizational stress and change. An interim treasures these experiences, like tattoos, scars, and trophies, and often refers to them to illustrate key points. Of course, a successful interim uses stories to show rather than tell, to illustrate rather than dictate; all this is done with appropriate discretion. Clients should be wary of an interim or colleague who uses a story as a predictor of success or as an example to be precisely copied. Organizations, economies, clients, products, finances, markets, people, countries – these all provide a deep pool of stories from which an interim draws as he or she helps clients through their specific circumstances. Drawing from these diverse experiences, an interim is equipped to share valuable insights with new clients and impact the evolution of culture within client organizations.

. . . .

An interim treasures experiences like tattoos, scars, and trophies, and often refers to them to illustrate key points.

. . . .

Integration can accommodate interpretation and transformation without nullifying the past or present. It is easier for an interim to make a difference by initially showing respect and acknowledgement for the present state. Most interims enjoy the diverse cultures in which he or she has worked. This isn't to say that there are no surprises. For example, there are still organizations where an interim is told to go "up the hierarchy" if he or she wants to communicate and influence. These organizational cultures have a strict interpretation of what it means to respect the cultural and organizational ladder. This contrasts with other organizations where for example the CEO welcomes direct conversations with employees, interims, and others.

It is essential that an interim integrates with the culture of an organization. This is discussed in detail in Chapter 5, which explores cultural savvy based on the SCILL Model©. An interim has an opportunity to expand the organization's culture. Most clients expect an interim to assess the impact of projects and leadership on the organization's culture. An interim leader leaves an organization with a sense that "the interim made things better around here".

Teams

Clients rarely expect an interim to be a lone wolf or intrepid fixer who does not integrate with other parts of the organization. Often, an interim immediately integrates with a leadership team because he or she is engaged in a "line position" rather than just a project role. This support from client leadership legitimizes an interim's leadership and influence. An interim demonstrates that he or she is a first-class colleague by investing time to build relationships. This is accomplished in many ways; an interim volunteers for activities, enjoys socializing with the rest of the team, wrestles in the mire of organizational challenges, and celebrates when the team achieves victories.

Some aspects of integrating into the leadership team are out of an interim's immediate control. Some clients consider a place in the inner sanctum as the privilege of those who have signed up to be a permanent part of the organization. In these instances, an interim has an opportunity rather than a closed door. By demonstrating gravitas and delivering results, and taking every opportunity to network with other leaders, an interim will eventually receive regular invitations to sit at the top table. In fact, an interim does not have the "right" to be part of a senior leadership team – it is earned.

When a client asks an interim to lead a team, there is an opportunity to integrate. Team members should feel an interim is their advocate and leader. An interim needs to deliver this with an acknowledgement that he or she is there to make a difference, and that this may involve changes to the team. An interim brings challenge and transformation along with advocacy.

. . . .

An interim brings challenge and transformation along with advocacy.

. . . .

In *The Trusted Advisor* David Maister points to three basic skills of a trusted advisor: "earning trust, giving advice effectively, and building relationships." These three skills are required of an interim to lead and integrate into the client team. The best balance for an interim with regards to team integration is to share the same challenges, values, and goals as the team, without compromising the leadership and courage needed to make changes. Often, an interim can work this out with craft, timing, and positive intent. This might include suggesting alternatives, creating new visions, and articulating creative strategies; these are always better than confrontation or hasty judgments. The fluctuations of organizational change present challenges for an interim's leadership of a team. The following example illustrates this:

Example: Team integration and organizational change

An interim leader inherited a team with a few great leaders. Some were in exactly the right role, others had personal ambitions to be in different roles, and others needed motivating to move to a role that suited them better. A critical part of the interim's role was to get to know each leader and to lead the assignment with the whole team. One leader on the team in particular was not the right fit in terms of experience and capability for the role she was being asked to fulfil. She had responsibilities for a function that the interim recommended be absorbed by another part of the operation. This meant that this team member no longer had a role. As part of discharging his responsibilities, the interim made a commitment to help this talented leader find a new role. Dealing with a team member who is fearful for his or her tenure is not an easy situation for an interim. Eventually the team member found a new role and moved on. The interim was both the good guy and bad guy during this transition, but the outcome worked for everyone on the team.

An interim must balance and manage his or her contribution as a team member and as an independent expert. Remaining vibrant and relevant is a challenge for an interim. Moving between clients is part of what makes an interim so effective, so becoming over-familiar with an organization can be a hindrance to effectiveness. An interim chooses diverse learning through multiple client and project experiences. This often means difficult decisions need to be made when the time comes for an interim to separate from a client. Often the client wants to keep an interim around rather than address issues in the ranks of the permanent leadership or have to consider a further change in the team. An interim's integration as a team member is a strength that can become a hindrance if prolonged. During the defined tenure of an interim's contract, relationships become strong, trust is mutual, and respect with a common purpose unites the interim and client's leadership and teams.

Projects

What are the operational expectations a client has of an interim as he or she embarks on a project? Managing projects requires coordination, control, and communication. A client is likely to experience the professionalism of an interim in this regard. An effective interim breaks a project into component parts, analyzes its resource requirements, and formulates a structured approach to project management. Because of an interim's experience with multiple assignments and leadership roles, the interim's insight into the demands for project discipline is usually well developed.

· ·

An interim breaks a project into component parts, analyzes its resource requirements, and formulates a structured approach.

· ·

It is not unusual for an interim to initiate building a comprehensive project plan to bring clarity to a project, even if the client does not have a formal methodology or established practice for doing this. An interim thrives on project management, knowing that the discipline and rigor of following a plan brings clarity and controlled delivery. Project management is an essential skill every interim needs to successfully deliver assignments.

Project Reporting

An interim leader is highly tuned to the need to provide detailed reporting to diverse stakeholder groups. Accountability and tracking are essential disciplines for an interim to keep clients updated on projects and expected outcomes.

An interim's discipline of accounting for results delivered on a project and subsequent invoices is a helpful backdrop to the overall pattern of working with a client. For most interims, this expectation is similar to consultancies who are required to justify their costs against time spent delivering against client projects. An interim often gets drawn into organizational activity —culture discussions, team meetings, and conferences — that is not directly tied to the interim's primary objectives. However, during these activities an effective interim takes note of how he or she adds value. It is a worthwhile objective for both the client and interim to always report on "value" – this defines the red thread throughout an interim's contribution. Whatever reporting requirement a client asks of an interim, he or she will always endeavor to adopt professional disciplines.

. . . .

Always report on "value" – this defines the red thread throughout an interim's contribution.

. . . .

A client may sometimes experience that an interim "over-reports", providing his or her chief sponsor with regular progress updates. Some organizations have lost their rigor for account-ability and regular reporting of progress and what may seem like over-reporting is a welcome, useful activity. Reporting, however, is not always the best use of an interim's time; for example, the client's infatuation with the interim's comprehensive reporting can distract time and energy from the fundamental benefits of hiring an interim. The client needs to harness an interim's expertise to maximize the tremendous value an interim brings. Once the interim has re-introduced the discipline of reporting, then he or she is more effective if not weighed down by administrative disciplines best carried out by others.

Project Communication

There is perhaps nothing more frustrating for a client than to have an expert who is unable to communicate effectively, especially within the framework of managing projects. Hiring an interim is an opportunity for the client to establish clear expectations about the desired style and cadence of communication. Effective communication often hinges on individual style preferences; an interim takes cues from the client organization's culture to execute communications that are appropriate and professional. An interim has developed a reputation as a leader and expert, accompanied with considerable savvy and gravitas—attributes that are essential to effective communication.

An interim is fluent in communications with all project stakeholders and recognizes their diverse needs. These include; engaging with the C-suite, keeping his or her sponsor aware of progress, motivating the team, and engaging every colleague with information and insight. In *The Trusted Advisor,*

David Maister summarizes the need for flexible approaches to communication:

> "The burden is on the advisor to quickly understand each individual client's preferred style of interaction, and to be sufficiently flexible to deal with him or her in the manner that the client finds most comfortable and effective."

An interim is required to communicate throughout a project lifecycle in a number of ways:

- Internal/external communication to gather research, assess best practice
- Communication with stakeholders to get buy-in for change
- Presentations to senior leadership, teams
- Communication with internal teams impacted by change
- Written communication
- Communication with external consultants, vendors

An added challenge for an interim is working virtually with a client. In fact, an interim may only occasionally venture onto client sites. When leading a virtual project, an interim needs to ensure that he or she understands the client and key leaders sufficiently through office visits, before taking the opportunity of leading and delivering projects virtually. Communicating progress, understanding issues, and motivating team members through virtual communication, is a significant skill that an interim needs to exercise.

Dembitz and Essinger state in *Breakthrough Consulting*:

"Technical expertise can be a substitute for interpersonal skills to some extent, but it is important to remember that much of the effectiveness of technical advice depends on how it is communicated, especially if, as is likely to be the case, the advice needs to be implemented or followed up by the client." This is indeed a lesson well learned by the client and the interim leader!

CHAPTER 16

The SCILL Model©
Assessment

Hiring an interim presents many of the same challenges as hiring for a senior leadership or C-level position. One of the most important considerations is ensuring that the right match is made between a prospective interim and client. The client and interim both seek a "win-win". The client needs to engage a resource who will deliver. An interim seeking a client engagement must be convinced that the assignment is the right fit; this sets the conditions for success and ensures that the interim will deliver a successful outcome.

How can a client and an interim assess whether an assignment is the right fit? This chapter provides a framework using the SCILL Model© assessment; a useful insight and tool for both clients and interims.

Sourcing an Interim: A Tool for Clients

Screening questions are helpful for a client to ask prior to an interview with an interim. The answers to the following questions will help narrow the field:

Ten Screening Questions for Clients Seeking an Interim:

1. Does the interim's CV contain a headline match with the client's need? Does page one of the CV indicate that the interim has had success in the discipline before?
2. Does the interim's CV indicate that he or she is:
   - an expert in his or her field, through significant previous assignments
   - an authority in his or her field, through education, publications, research
   - current in his or her field, through recent contracts

3. How credible and relevant are the clients that the interim has worked with? If the client is a large international corporate organization, it is helpful for the interim to have had similar experiences.
4. Does the interim's CV demonstrate and quantify actual results as well as areas of expertise? Evidence is essential.
5. Does the interim align with the client's organization? A CV that centers on academic or even professional hyperbole might mean that the interim is not well-suited to a pragmatic, gloves-off organization. A CV that doesn't mention "culture" might mean the interim is not a great match for an organization in which culture is a major characteristic of the way it functions.
6. How does the interim agency speak about the individual? The agency should offer evidence of strong recommendation and affinity with the interim.
7. Do references and recommendations leave the client with no doubt that the interim is a class-act and would do a great job for the client?
8. Does the interim have professional credentials and

certifications to match his or her project successes?

9. Has the interim demonstrated agility by succeeding in client environments that cover different industry sectors and geographies?

10. Do previous client projects indicate that the interim has operated at the appropriate senior level to match the prospective client environment?

It may be that the client gains satisfactory answers to the questions above through the reassurance of the interim agency. Otherwise, an introductory telephone interview between the client and interim is recommended before moving to the next stage.

If the client has a positive profile of the interim based on answers to the above questions, the next move is to interview the interim. If the client has a gut sense about the interim and some of the criteria above do not land in the right place, more exploration is needed.

In some cases, an interim is just getting into this field of work and might be a great match; further exploration will reveal this. In another scenario, an interim may be a leader recently released from his or her previous organization. In this case, a client needs to find out the reasons why. Some reasons, such as downsizing, M&A, or strategic redirection, are legitimate. Being laid off doesn't disqualify a candidate; in fact, it can redefine and strengthen such an interim. An occasional red flag to be wary of is motivation; if an interim has chosen this career simply to bump up his or her pension this will not make for stellar performance.

How can a client assess an interim and construct an interview plan? The questions below are aligned to the SCILL Model©, and provide a template based on the SCILL attributes: Savvy, Critical, Impact, Leadership, Legacy. The answers, even to a selection of the questions, will illustrate the interim's strengths and motivations, and combined with other information such as references, will predict his or her success. The SCILL Model© assessment also helps determine the credibility of an interim, and how effectively he or she interprets the role as a catalyst for the client who is framing the interim assignment.

In considering the questions below, a client should also assess a prospective interim with the GREAT competencies in mind. How does he or she show up? What are his or her character traits? Does his or her temperament support the client's culture? Does he or she impress and inspire with confidence? A combination of GREAT competency assessment, within the framework of the SCILL Model© , provides an excellent platform for considering the suitability of an interim for a client project.

Assessment Questions for Clients

Savvy
1. Can you please give an example of how your initial insight into an organization impacted the way you addressed an interim assignment?
2. Describe some of the techniques you have used to understand the context of a client organization and how best to deliver an interim assignment.
3. Can you illustrate through a specific client relationship how you have built your reputation and credibility within the first month of an interim assignment?

4. Can you give an example of how a personal relationship you built within a client organization helped you to deliver your assignment?

5. Describe how the culture of a client organization impacted the way you approached an interim assignment.

6. Please give an example of a challenge you faced with a client organization's culture and how you adapted to it.

Critical

1. Can you describe an interim assignment for which you were responsible and that had the greatest impact on your client's business strategy?

2. Describe the outcomes of an interim assignment that addressed a client organization's crisis, growth, or change. How did you measure these outcomes?

3. Can you provide an example of how your responsibility for an interim assignment integrated into a broader client strategic initiative?

4. Describe an interim assignment where you have had to engage others in a critical activity. How did you go about this?

5. What personal attributes do you have that give a client confidence to trust you with a critical project? How have these served you well with a previous client?

6. Describe an interim project where you have had to deliver fast results, and where these results were critical to the client.

Impact
1. What is the most challenging question you have been asked by a client and how did you respond to it?
2. Describe an occasion when your recommendations to expand or change the scope of an interim assignment has added greater value to a client.
3. Can you describe how you have motivated others as part of a project to make a significant change to the client's business?
4. What would you say is the greatest way you can add value to a client? Please provide an example when you did this.
5. Describe an interim assignment that didn't have the impact you had hoped for. What would you have done differently?

Leadership
1. Can you give an example of something you have done between client assignments to keep yourself relevant as an interim leader?
2. Describe an occasion when your experience on previous projects has specifically helped you to deliver a client assignment.
3. Illustrate, using a previous client, how you have influenced the evolution of an organization's strategy or culture.
4. What would you regard as your greatest leadership strength? How has this been effective in a previous client assignment?

5. Please describe an occasion where your personal leadership had a transformational impact on a client organization and key stakeholders.

Legacy
1. Can you give an example of a client relationship that you maintained following completion of an assignment?
2. What would you say is your most memorable interim assignment and why?
3. Describe the interim assignment that has had the greatest impact on a client's business.
4. What is your core motivation as an interim? Please provide an example of how this has impacted a previous client relationship.

The SCILL Model© Assessment is a double-edged tool; a client benefits from it in hiring an interim leader and an interim can use it for self-evaluation. The questions provide a good framework for an interim seeking to skillfully articulate a wide range of client experiences. Certainly, the questions are a tool for an interim who wants to prepare for a client interview. However, an unhelpful by-product of this can be rehearsed, even slick, responses instead of authentic answers. It is paramount for an interim to be tuned into the context, individuals, and organizational culture during an interview.

Validating an Interim Career: A Tool for Interims

What attributes make for a successful interim? These questions are aligned to the SCILL Model© and provide a template based on the SCILL attributes: Savvy, Critical, Impact, Leadership,

Legacy. They are designed for an individual who is seeking to begin an interim leader career and are a useful revision for an interim preparing for an interview with a client.

Assessment Questions for Interims

Savvy
1. Am I quick to assess situations or do I prefer to spend more time researching and validating?
2. Is my insight into a situation or a person usually proven right?
3. Do I have broad experience from working in different organizations, across sectors and geographies?
4. Am I an expert in my field, proven by my academic and career achievements?
5. Am I able to adapt quickly to different cultures, clients, and projects?
6. Do I see organizations as systemic and understand the impact of different activities on various aspects of the organization?
7. Am I self-motivated and self-reliant in my ability to get things done?
8. Do I build productive relationships and have an extensive professional network?
Critical
1. Do I thrive on major challenges or am I more comfortable in steady, predictable environments?
2. Have I delivered projects with significant strategic and financial implications?
3. Do I regularly get asked to deliver transformational and other critical projects?

4. Am I motivated by responsibility and accountability?
5. Do I regularly deliver projects on time, to quality, and within budget?

Impact
1. Do I thrive on change?
2. Is my main reason for working in my field to make a difference to as many people and organizations as I can? Is this why I want to be an interim?
3. Do I usually get things done faster than others?
4. Does the scale of a challenge inspire me?
5. Do I relish moving from one organization to another with reasonable frequency to deliver projects?

Leadership
1. Have I worked at C-Suite level or Head of Function level in one or many organizations?
2. Am I inspired when leading others to deliver major projects? Are others inspired by me?
3. Am I the master of my own career, motivated to build networks for contract opportunities, and to use downtime constructively?
4. Do I often find myself giving proposals to senior leadership?
5. Do I have a bank of credible advocates willing to give excellent references?
6. Have I often found myself delivering proposals beyond my immediate scope of work?
7. Am I comfortable with the risk of not having steady work – both financially and emotionally? (Does this also fit with my personal circumstances, e.g. family?)

Legacy
1. Do I have a track-record of success?
2. Do I have a history of contract extensions with clients or significant roles held with employers?
3. Do I take pride in the changes I have made to organizations and the impact I have had on people?
4. Do I care more about my achievements than my employment longevity?

There are many self-assessment, personality, and career assessments on the market, but none are uniquely geared to the career of an interim leader. The SCILL Model© Assessment questions provide a template – a starting point for the journey. This book provides extensive information, insights, case studies, examples, and resources for a professional seeking an interim career. It is also valuable to connect with one or more of the agencies listed in the Resources section of this book.

Future Outlook for Interim Leaders

The need for interim leaders is growing. Senior leaders are more aware of the significant value that an interim leader brings to organizations in accelerating growth and transformation. Traditional approaches to leadership are inadequate for modern organizations, and as Marshall Goldsmith suggests in his book of the same title, "*What got you here won't get you there*" – old habits that once brought success are now delaying progress.

Clients need high-caliber, experienced, and dynamic leaders who take ownership of major projects, build relationships, and deliver results. An interim leader is a resource that is more readily available than ever. In fact, many experienced leaders and subject-matter experts are taking charge of their careers by becoming interim leaders — today's gig leaders. An interim leader plays to his or her strengths, delivers high-value results to clients, and creates a portfolio career that works to both the interim's and client's advantage in the growing gig economy.

Resources & Notes

Resources

Interim Agencies and Associations

A selection of interim agencies is included below. A comprehensive list can be found on the Internet. Professional networks for interims leaders are available through organizations such as the Association of Interim Executives and the Institute of Interim Management.

USA

Association of Interim Executives

https://www.interimexecs.org/

Boyden US Interim Management

https://www.boydeninterim.com/us-interim/

ES Interims

http://www.esinterims.com/

Cerius Executives

https://ceriusexecutives.com/

Executives Unlimited

https://www.executivesunlimited.com/

PwC Talent Exchange

https://talentexchange.pwc.com/

UK

Boyden UK Interim Management

https://www.boydeninterim.co.uk/uk-interim/

IIM

https://iim.org.uk/international/

Odgers Interim

https://www.odgersinterim.com/

Interim Partners

https://www.interimpartners.com/

Penna

http://penna.com/

BIE

https://www.bie-executive.com/interim-management

Alium Partners

http://www.aliumpartners.com/

Executives Online

http://www.executivesonline.com/

EUROPE

DDIM (Germany)

https://www.ddim.de/

Boyden Interim Management Germany

https://www.boydeninterim.de/de/germany-interim/contact/index.html

IIM (Italy)

http://www.temporary-management.com/iim/index_ita.htm

SIM (Poland)

http://www.stowarzyszenieim.org/

AIM (Spain)

http://interimspain.org/en/

DSIM (Switzerland)

http://www.dsim.ch/

AUSTRALIA

Australasian Interim Executive Association

https://www.aiea.org.au/

Executive Interim Management

http://www.eim.com.au/

Notes

Alasdair Drysdale, *The Interim Director*, (Oxford: Management Books 2000, 2015)

Alex Dembitz and James Essinger, *Breakthrough Consulting*, (Harlow: Financial Times Prentice Hall, 2000)

Charles Besondy and Paul Travis, *Leadership On Demand*, (Round Rock: LOD Publishing LLC, 2008)

Charles Darwin, *The Origin of Species*, (New York: Bantam Dell, 1999)

Charles Handy, *The Age of Unreason*, (Boston: Harvard Business School Press, 1990)

Charles Handy, *The Empty Raincoat*, (London: Arrow Business Books, 1994)

Charles Handy, *The Second Curve*, (London: Random House Books, 2015)

Daniel Goleman, *Emotional Intelligence*, (London: Bloomsbury Publishing, 1996)

Daniel Goleman, Richard Boyatzis and Annie McKee, *Primal Leadership*, (Boston: Harvard Business Review Press, 2013)

David Clutterbuck, *Everyone Needs a Mentor – Third Edition*, (London: The Chartered Institute of Personnel and Development, 2001)

David Clutterbuck and Des Dearlove, *The Interim Manager*, (London: Financial Times Pitman Publishing, 1999)

David Corbett with Richard Higgins, *Portfolio Life*, (San Francisco: Jossey-Bass, 2007)

David H. Maister, *The Trusted Advisor*, (New York: Free Press, 2000)

David Ulrich, Norm Smallwood and Kate Sweetman, *The Leadership Code*, (Boston: Harvard Business Press, 2008)

Dennis Russell and Ian Daniell, *Interim Management,* (Salcombe: Aveton Books, 2005)

Diane Mulcahy, *The Gig Economy*, (New York, Amacom, 2017)

Edgar Schein, *Organizational Culture and Leadership -Second Edition*, (San Francisco: Jossey-Bass, 1992)

Erik De Haan, *Relational Coaching*, (Chichester, John Wiley & Sons Ltd, 2008)

Esther Cameron and Mike Green, *Making Sense of Change Management* -Third Edition, (London: Kogan Page, 2012)

Giles Hutchins, *Future Fit*, (Seattle: CreateSpace Independent Publishing Platform, 2016)

James Kouzes and Barry Posner, *The Leadership Challenge – Fifth Edition*, (San Francisco: Jossey-Bass, 2012)

Jim Collins, *Good to Great*, (New York: Harper Business, 2001)

Jim Collins and Jerry Porras, *Built to Last*, (New York: Harper Business, 1994)

John Kotter, *Leading Change*, (Boston: Harvard Business Review Press, 2012)

John Kotter, *Accelerate (XLR8)*, (Boston: Harvard Business Review Press, 2014)

Luc De Brabandere, *The Forgotten Half of Change*, (Chicago: Dearborn Trade Publishing, 2005)

Marion McGovern and Dennis Russell, *A New Brand of Expertise*, (Woburn: Butterworth Heinemann, 2001)

Marshall Goldsmith, *What Got You Here Won't Get You There*, (London: Profile Books, 2007)

Patrick Lencioni, *The Advantage*, (San Francisco: Jossey-Bass, 2012)

Peter Drucker, *The Effective Executive*, (New York: HarperCollins, 2006)

Philip Doggett, *The Secrets of Interim Management*, (Aylesbury, self-published, 2017)

Richard Lindenmuth, *The Outside the Box Executive*, (Raleigh-Durham: Publishing Unleashed, 2013)

Rob Goffee and Gareth Jones, *Why Should Anyone Be Led by YOU?*, (Boston: Harvard Business Review Press, 2006)

Robert H. Schaffer, *High Impact Consulting*, (San Francisco: Jossey-Bass Publishers, 1997)

Ronald Heifetz, Marty Linsky and Alexander Grashow, *The Practice of Adaptive Leadership* (Boston: Harvard Business Press, 2009)

Taylor Pearson, *The End of Jobs*, (Austin: Lioncrest Publishing, 2015)

William Bridges, *Job Shift*, (Cambridge: Perseus Books, 1994)

William Bridges, *Managing Transitions*, (London: Nicholas Brealey Publishing, 1995)

Articles & Surveys

Deloitte Human Capital Trends, (New York: Deloitte University Press, 2017)

When Your Employees Know More Than You, (Boston, Harvard Business Review, July 20, 2010)

IIM Interim Management Survey, (West Byfleet: Institute of Interim Management, 2014)

"Building and Retaining Global Talent: Towards 2002", Mike Johnson

The Rise and Nature of Alternative Work Arrangements in the United States, 1995-2015, Lawrence F. Katz and Alan B. Krueger, (March 29th, 2016)

Business Guides

Confederation of British Industry, *Interim Executive Management*, (London: Caspian Publishing and BIE Interim Executive, 2004)

Interviews

Bob Jordan, CEO, Interim Execs, Chicago, Ill., interviewed by the author, August 14, 2017

Bill Flannery, Partner, Boyden, Pittsburgh, Pa., interviewed by the author, August 7, 2017

Personal Communications

Interim Client Case Studies (Chapters 4 - 9), email correspondence with author (March – June 2017), confidentiality requested;

Interim Client Examples (Chapter 2), email correspondence with author (March – June 2017), confidentiality requested;

Interim Leader Case Studies (Chapter 3), email correspondence with author (March – June 2017), confidentiality requested;

Interim leader and client examples cited throughout the book: drawn from author's experiences;